A Handbook of Canadian LEGAL Terminology
Revised and Updated

William J. Flynn

Stoddart

Copyright © 1976, 1981, 1986 William J. Flynn

All rights reserved. No part of this publication may be reproduced or transmitted in any form or by any means, electronic or mechanical, including photography, recording, or any information storage and retrieval system, without permission in writing from the publisher.

First published in 1976 by
new press

Revised edition published in 1981 by
General Publishing Co. Limited

Published in 1986 by
Stoddart Publishing Co. Limited
34 Lesmill Road
Toronto, Ontario
M3B 2T6

Canadian Cataloguing in Publication Data

Flynn, William J.
  A handbook of Canadian legal terminology

ISBN 0-7737-5107-6

1. Law — Canada — Terms and phrases. I. Title.

KE183.F69   1987   349.71'01'4   C86-094906-0

Cover design: Newton/Frank
Cover photograph: Peter Paterson

Printed in Canada

A Handbook of Canadian LEGAL Terminology
Revised and Updated

A Handbook of Canadian LEGAL Terminology
Revised and Updated

PREFACE

As societies become more complex, the need for legal knowledge becomes more important if the individual is to function effectively within the society. In the past, people have relied almost entirely on the knowledge of a few highly trained professionals for legal counsel and advice. Today, more people are taking an active interest in the legal processes that affect them in their daily lives.

A Handbook of Canadian Legal Terminology, now newly revised, has been compiled to bridge the gap between the legal profession and the general public. This practical, handly compendium presents the lay person with simplified interpretations of the most common legal terms used in contracts, other legal documents, public policy statements and the media. Para-legal workers, legal secretaries, police officers, business people, social workers, students and many others will find it a valuable addition to their personal or professional libraries. Even the professional lawyer often needs a handy, quick reference to legal usage and spelling.

In order to keep this work non-technical, yet accurate, what is presented here is the author's interpretation of the terms. Obviously certain words and phrases — particularly in Latin — are specific in definition, and the author wishes to acknowledge the many legal books wherein these words are found time and again.

A

a fortiori: All the more; from a stronger reason.

a priori: An argument which has only a remote bearing on the issue.

a vinculo matrimonii: From the bond of matrimony.

ab initio: At the outset; from the beginning. *Void ab initio*; void from the beginning.

ab intestato: From an intestate. Succession *ab intestato* means the succession to the property of a person dying intestate. See **intestate**.

abatement: When assets are insufficient to meet a debt, a proportionate deduction of the amount owing is made.

abdicate: To give up a right or a responsibility; to give up a governmental position or a throne.

abet: To encourage another in the commission of a crime; to present aid actually or by implication.

abortion: An intentional miscarriage of the contents of the womb before termination of the period of gestation. Abortion is legal in some jurisdictions under specific conditions.

abrogate: To repeal; to give up or annul.

absolute: Complete without condition (*e.g.*, in the case of divorce). See **decree nisi**.

absolute liability: Liability that arises and is imposed on a person regardless of the situation leading to the liability.

A

abstract of title: A summary of all recorded instruments constituting the title to land.

abutting property: Real property which adjoins or touches another property.

acceptance: Agreement to an offer in a contract made by express words or conduct, not to be confused with mere intention.

accepting service: Where a solicitor for a defendant accepts service of a writ or other court process on behalf of a client.

accessory: One connected with an offence who is not the main person, nor present at its performance. An accessory before the fact is one who counsels, orders, or procures another to commit a crime. An accessory after the fact is one who harbors, assists or protects another after the other has committed an offence.

accommodation indorser: One who co-signs a bill or note without consideration and becomes liable should the other party fail to pay.

accomplice: One who joins with another in the commission of a criminal offence.

accord and satisfaction: The payment of an agreed amount when there is a disagreement over what is due.

accrue: To arise. Dower rights in land accrue for a woman on the death of her husband.

accused: The defendant in a criminal trial.

acquiesence: Consent between parties either express or implied.

A

acquit: To set free from a charge by judgment of the court.

act of God: An unusual, unforeseeable occurrence arising from natural causes (*e.g.*, a hurricane or earthquake). See **vis major**.

action: The right of a plaintiff to prosecute a defendant for an injury done, or damage caused. See **plaintiff**; **defendant**.

actual cash value: The reasonable cash price for which property could be sold. In some insurance claims, the value at the time of loss.

actus reus: An act by which an offence is committed.

ad hoc: For this purpose. An official appointed to, or by, the court for a special reason.

ad idem: Agreement on an important issue. Very important in contract law. See **consensus ad idem**.

ad infinitum: To continue on without end; indefinitely.

ad interim: In the meantime.

ad litem: For the suit. A guardian *ad litem* is appointed by the court to appear on behalf of an infant.

ad valorem: According to the value. With respect to a duty, or tax, on property.

ademption: A revocation of a bequest in a will by a subsequent act of the testator.

adjourn: To put off the hearing of a case until a future time, usually at the court's discretion. See **sine die**.

A

adjudge: To make a judicial decision.

adjudication: A judgment rendered in equity; to determine that a debtor is bankrupt.
The final judgment of a court.

administration: The distribution of a deceased's estate according to law.

administrative law: The law regarding administration of the state; with legislative or judicial powers.

administrator/administratrix: A man/woman to whom administration of an estate is granted.

admissions: In evidence, testimony in which an individual charged admits the truth of a fact presented to the court.

adoption: A judicial process whereby the rights and obligations of the natural parents are voided and are vested in the adoptive parents. The relationship is then as if the child was the adoptive parent's natural born child.

adultery: Voluntary sexual intercourse of a married person with a person of the opposite sex other than the offender's husband or wife.

adversary system: The current system in the courts of an accusation against one person (*defendant*) by the plaintiff seeking decision by a court.

adverse possession: Where one person holds property by title and another person claims to be the rightful owner of the property by another title, the possession of the former is said to be adverse of the latter. See **prescription**.

A

affidavit: A statement in writing and under oath sworn before someone with authority to administer the oath.

affiliation: A process whereby a woman applies for a court order to declare that a man alleged by her to be the father of her child is indeed the father. See **putative (father)**.

affinity: A relationship by marriage rather than by blood. See **consanguinity**.

affirm: To make a statement under oath; to confirm a former law or judgment (*e.g.*, an appeal court affirms the judgment of a lower court).

agent: An individual who acts for a principal in relations with a third party within the terms of powers specified by the principal.

agent of necessity: One who pledges the credit of another in an emergency (*e.g.*, a deserted wife pledging husband's credit for necessaries).

agreement: Where two or more persons express agreement in an issue. In contract law, a promise is made by one party and agreed to by another party.

alias: Another name, other than his own, used by a person usually to deceive another as to his actual identity.

alibi: Elsewhere. To offer an excuse. When an accused person attempts to show that he (or she) could not have committed the alleged offence because he (or she) was elsewhere at the time, the defence is called an alibi.

alien: A person who is not a citizen of the particular country in which he resides. See **naturalization**.

A

alienation: The transfer of real or personal property to another.

alimony: Periodic payments for support of a divorced or separated spouse, made under a court order. See **maintenance.**

alio intuitu: A purpose other than the apparent one.

all fours: A phrase signifying that the case at issue is in total agreement with a previous decision.

allegation: A statement by a plaintiff which the plaintiff undertakes to prove.

a.m.: *Ante meridiem*, before noon.

amalgamation: The union by merger of two or more corporations.

ambiguity: Uncertainty as to the meaning of a written or oral statement.

amicus curiae: A friend of the court. A by-stander (*e.g.,* barrister, counsellor) who gives information on points of law, of which the judge is doubtful or mistaken.

amnesty: An act of government that pardons offences.

ancillary: Additional; auxiliary.

animus furandi: An intention to steal.

animus manendi: An intention to remain; a point to be settled in ascertaining a person's domicile.

annul: To make void (*e.g.,* a marriage); to destroy the force of a thing (*e.g.,* a contract).

A

ante litem motam: Before litigation was contemplated.

ante-date: To date an instrument before the day of its execution.

appeal: A complaint to a superior court claiming justice was not done by an inferior court. The complainant is the appellant, the other party is the respondent.

appellant: The party complaining in an appeal; the plaintiff. See **respondent**.

appurtenance: Something outside of land but belonging to it and adding to one's enjoyment of it (*e.g.*, the right to use a water way).

arbitrator: A person selected to decide a disagreement out of court.

arraignment: To bring a person charged with a criminal offence before the court to be tried. See **indictment**.

arson: The deliberate burning of another's property.

articles: The separate clauses of a written agreement.

ascendent: In estate law one who is a parent, grandparent, etc. of the person who has died. See **descendent**.

assault: A physical or verbal threat to harm another without actually carrying out the threat. A civil or criminal action may arise. See **battery**.

assign: To transfer to another all right, title and interest in property.

A

assumption of mortgage: In taking title to property, a grantee assumes personal liability for an existing debt.

assured: The person an insurance company agrees to indemnify against certain perils.

attachment: A process whereby assets can be held pending results of litigation.

attest: To witness a signature; to affirm to be true.

attorney-at-law: One who is appointed to take the place of another to handle legal problems. In common law, an attorney may give advice and prepare legal documents but may not plead in court. A barrister must proceed to plead in court. In most jurisdictions, an attorney encompasses both functions. See **barrister; counsel; lawyer; solicitor.**

Attorney-General: In the U.K., the main counsel for the Crown. In the U.S.A., the head of the Department of Justice and in each state, the chief law officer and head of the legal department. See **Solicitor-General.**

attorney-in-fact: One who holds a power of attorney as an agent of another.

attractive nuisance doctrine: One who leaves something dangerous to a child on his or her premises in a position and place that may attract children (*e.g.,* an unfenced swimming pool) owes a duty to exercise reasonable care to protect them against danger.

A

autrefois acquit: A plea by which an accused pleads that he has already been tried and acquitted of the same offence in order to stop criminal prosecution.

authorized capital: The number and kind of shares a corporation may sell; c.f., a share inventory.

autrefois convict: A special plea by the defence alleging that the accused has already been tried and convicted of the same criminal offence.

averment: An offer to prove; proof of a plea. A technical name for the allegations made in a pleading.

B

bail bond: A guarantee, usually money, given to a court assuring that an accused will appear, when required, to answer the charge. If the accused does not appear, the bond is forfeited to the court.

bailee: A person to whom goods are entrusted.

bailiff: An officer of an inferior court who functions at a level similar to a sheriff in a superior court. See **sheriff**.

bailment: A delivery of goods or personal property from the bailor to the bailee for some purpose, and to be returned to the bailor after the purpose of the bailment is complete.

bailor: A person who entrusts goods to a bailee.

bankrupt: A debtor who, unable to pay his debts, assigns his estate to a trustee to be divided equally among his creditors, according to the law and by order of the court.

bankruptcy: A judicial proceeding to distribute assets of an insolvent person to his creditors. The bankrupt is then relieved of further liability even if the creditors receive less than whole recompense.

barrister: One admitted to the bar in the U.K.; those who plead in court. See **attorney; counsel; lawyer; solicitor**.

battery: The striking, hitting, touching, or laying hold of another person, however slight. See **assault**.

bench: The judge or the court.

B

bench warrant: A court order issued for the arrest of an accused who does not appear for trial as required, or a properly subpoenaed witness who does not appear as required.

benchers: The governing officers of a Law Society or the equivalent.

beneficiary: A person to whom something is given, usually by will; the *cestui que trust* in a trust relationship. See **cestui que trust**.

bequeath: A gift with reference to personalty in a will. See **devise**.

bequest: A gift of personal property in a will; a legacy.

bestiality: Any manner of carnal knowledge by a man or a woman with a beast.

bigamy: The offence of marrying a second time knowing that a former marriage is undissolved or that a former husband or wife is still living.

bill of exchange: An unconditional order in writing addressed by one party (the drawer) to another (the drawee) signed by the person giving it, requiring the person to whom it is addressed to pay on demand, or at fixed time, a sum of money. It may also be payable to the order of a specific person or to the bearer (the payee).

bill of lading: A document containing a description of goods to be shipped. It is directed to the shipper, signed by a public carrier and is evidence of the contract and a receipt of the goods.

B

binder: An interim agreement covering an insured party until issuance of the actual insurance policy.

blackmail: To extort money by threat.

bona fide: In good faith (*e.g.*, a *bona fide* contract).

bona vacantia: Goods without actual owner or legal claimant. The goods then vest to the government.

breach of contract: Refusal or failure to carry out a contract as promised.

breach of duty: An omission of a legal or moral duty (*e.g.*, the failure to properly perform a trust position).

brief: A short or summarized writing of the pleadings used or to be used in litigation before the court.

burden of proof: The duty to prove one's case. The plaintiff must prove his case on the balance of probabilities. When this is done, the onus shifts to the defendant to disprove the allegations. In criminal law, the burden is on the prosecution to prove guilt beyond a reasonable doubt. Also called onus of proof.

burglary: Breaking and entering into the premises of another with intent to commit a felony.

by-laws: Rules and regulations adopted by a corporation or association to regulate its internal operations; the ordinances of a town.

C

c.i.f.: Cost, insurance, freight. Prices are quoted "c.i.f." from a particular place and include all costs up to delivery at the indicated destination. See **f.o.b.**.

cannabis sativa: A narcotic including cannabis resin; marijuana and its derivitives.

capacity: The ability at law to effect contracts on one's own behalf. The age of majority or capacity varies by jurisdiction and may range from 18 to 21. See **sui juris**.

capias: A writ addressed to the sheriff whereby process is issued against an accused person after indictment.

capita, distribution per: The division of an intestate's property, each claimant sharing in equal degree of kindred to the deceased and not as a representative of another. See **stirpes, distribution per**.

capital punishment: Punishment of death.

carrier: One who carries goods for hire for another. In insurance, refers to the insurance company itself.

cashier's check: An order to pay money drawn by an officer of a bank and paid out of the bank's own funds.

causa causans: The effective cause; literally the final link in a chain of causation.

causa sine qua non: The cause without which nothing would have happened. A cause but for which *causa causans* could not have occurred.

C

causa mortis: Because of death. See **donatio mortis causa**.

cause of action: The basis by which one person may sue another.

caution: A warning to all, when registered against land, that the cautioner has a claim against said land.

caveat: Let him beware. A warning. Similar to a caution. A warning to third parties that the caveator has an interest in a matter before the courts, or in some systems relevant to land.

caveat emptor: Let the buyer beware. A buyer of goods does so at his or her own risk.

cede: To assign or transfer.

certified check: A check guaranteeing the bank will pay the payee funds on presentation.

certified copy: A copy of a document that is certified as true and signed by the party who holds the original.

certiorari: A writ by a superior court wishing to be better informed; to inquire into the validity of an inferior court proceeding.

cessation: To cease action: *e.g.*, to stop proceedings in an action.

cestui que trust: A person for whose benefit a trust is created.

chain of title: Title to land from original patent to present date.

C

champerty or champarty: The process of a third party maintaining or financing a person in a suit on the condition there be a sharing of the property, real or personal, when recovered.

change of venue: To remove an action from one jurisdiction to another in an attempt to assure a trial free of local prejudice.

charge: A mortgage registered in land title system jurisdictions; a formal criminal accusation.

chattels: Personal property other than real property which is movable and tangible. Chattels real are interests in land less than freehold; leasehold interest.

check: A negotiable instrument ordering a bank to pay another person out of the drawer's own funds.

check-off system: The collection of union dues by having the employer make deductions from the employee's wages.

chicanery: To use deception or trickery to delude another into a position detrimental to his interest.

chose: A thing. A chose in action is the right to recover money or damages in a legal action. A chose in possession is a thing of which the owner is in actual possession or custody.

circumstantial evidence: Circumstances from which a fact may reasonably be presumed. As opposed to direct or positive evidence.

citation: The quotation of, and reference to, legal cases and authorities in courts of law; calling upon a party to an action to appear before the court.

C

civil law: Other than criminal, religious, or military law.

claim: Exercising a right of interest in something in another's possession. See **statement of claim**.

class action: A proceeding before the courts by a plaintiff in his own right and on behalf of others with similar complaints arising from the same situation.

clean hands: A doctrine in equity that says, "He who comes to equity must come with clean hands." A plaintiff must be free of taint with respect to the subject of his claim.

closed shop: An agreement that a worker must be a member of a union in good standing in order to be employed.

closing: A meeting between vendor and purchaser of land, usually through their lawyers to finalize transfer of land and funds therefor.

cloud on title: That which impairs validity of title to real property.

coca (erythroxylon): A narcotic containing coca leaves and cocaine.

codicil: A supplement explaining or altering part of a will. It must be executed in the same manner as the will itself.

co-executor: One who is named by a testator to be a joint executor with one or more others.

cognizance: Judicial knowledge requiring action.

C

cohabitation: Living together as husband and wife, legally married or in a common law union.

co-insurance: A clause in an insurance policy providing for sharing of a loss between the insurer and the insured.

collateral: Related to the main point, or matter, under consideration. Not part of the main issue.
Property or other interest transferred to another to secure a loan.

collateral issue: In a criminal prosecution, an issue arising out of a plea which does not relate to the accused's guilt or innocence.

collusion: An agreement between two or more persons to defraud another. Often used in divorce.

common form probate: A grant of probate by the court, with little formality, in an *ex parte* application of the executors. Probate in common form is revocable. See **probate**.

common law: The law based on a system of English law. Originally based on the common customs of the country.

company: A group of persons associated for reasons of business or trade with a view of profit. See **corporation**.

compensatory damages: Actual damages or an amount as close to the actual loss as possible. See **punitive damages**.

competency: The law of evidence. The characteristics which make a witness legally able to give testimony in court.

complaint: To charge a person with a crime.

C

conciliation: A process, usually in labor, whereby disputes are settled without litigation.

condition precedent: A condition that must be met before a contract becomes operative.

condition subsequent: A future event which when it occurs concludes a contract.

condominium: A system of individual ownership in land of a specific unit of a multi-unit structure. The common ownership of certain parts is referred to as the common elements.

condonation: To forgive voluntarily one's spouse for an act which might be a ground for divorce.

confession: In criminal law, the accused's voluntary admission of guilt to an offence with which he or she is charged.

conflict of laws: The dissimilarity between laws of different jurisdictions (*e.g.,* between states or countries).

conjoints: Persons who are married to each other.

conjugal: Of the married state.

connivance: To deliberately agree to an act by another person which one would normally resist (*e.g.,* one spouse permitting the other to commit adultery to gain a divorce. If proven, the divorce may not be granted by the court.) See **collusion.**

consanguinity: Relationship by blood. See **affinity.**

consensus ad idem: An agreement between all parties as to intent and terms. Necessary for a valid contract. See **meeting of minds.**

C

conservator: A person appointed by the court to manage the interests of a person who is not competent in law to manage his or her own interest. See **guardian.**

consideration: Something of value which must pass between the parties to a contract.

consignee: A person to whom goods are consigned by a consignor.

consignment: The delivering of goods; the goods themselves.

consignor: A person who consigns goods.

consortium: The right of a husband or wife to the companionship, help and affection of the other.

contribution: The payment of a proportionate share of liability by all who are equally liable.

contributory negligence: A sharing of responsibility by a plaintiff because of his own negligence.

construction: Interpretation of statutes to decide what effect words in the statute might have in court.

constructive notice: Notice that is inferred by law wherein a person is deemed to have had information or knowledge of a fact.

construe: The process of determining the application of a provision in a statute. See **construction.**

consummation: To complete something (*e.g.,* the completion of a marriage by sexual intercourse).

contempt of court: An act that reduces the dignity of the court, or hinders or disobeys its orders.

C

contingent legacy: Something bequeathed subject to a contingency (*e.g.,* that the legatee be at least 30 years old in order to receive the bequest).

contra bonos mores: Against good morals.

contra pacem: Against the peace.

contract: An agreement between persons of capacity to do a lawful thing for value.

conveyance: The transfer of title to land from one person to another.

copyright: An intangible legal right in an intellectual work usually for the life of the author and fifty years.

co-respondent: One who is accused of adultery with a person who is being sued for divorce.

corollary relief: An addition to a judgment arising from the judgment itself (*e.g.,* support payments arising from a divorce).

coroner's jury: A jury called to determine the cause, place and date of death caused by violence or under suspicious circumstances.

corporation: A business venture by one or more persons creating a legal entity which in itself is considered to be a legal person.

corporeal: That which exists in a material sense. A building is corporeal, its rental is incorporeal.

corpus delicti: The body of the wrong. In evidence, this signifies that a crime has occurred (*e.g.,* a death has been caused in a criminal way).

C

corpus juris civilis: The body of civil law.

correlative: Things in a reciprocal relationship to one another; the existence of one suggests the existence of the other. Rights and obligations are correlative.

corroborate: To add support to a thing by additional evidence.

costs: An allowance given to the successful party in litigation for expenses.

counsel: A barrister in the U.K. In the U.S.A., all attorneys or lawyers pleading before the courts. See **attorney; barrister; lawyer; solicitor**.

counsellor-at-law: A lawyer or attorney-at-law in the U.S.A.

counterclaim: A claim made by a defendant in answer to the claim of a plaintiff.

counts: Individual allegations of a plaintiff, if proven, could be separate causes of action. See **seriatum.**

court: The judge; a judicial tribunal; the place where justice is administered.

cousin german: A first cousin.

covenant: An agreement or promise in a legal document that something is done or shall be done or as to the truth of certain facts.

credibility: A quality in a witness that suggests that the testimony given should be believed.

C

cremation: The burning of human remains to ash in order to hygienically dispose of them.

criminal proceeding: A judicial proceeding fixing guilt and seeking punishment as a remedy.

Crown prosecutor: One who appears on behalf of the Crown in Canada and the U.K. in a criminal prosecution. See **District Attorney**.

culpa: Negligence or fault.

culpable: A breach of legal duty; fault as opposed to guilt. Culpable homicide includes murder, manslaughter or infanticide.

custom: Habits and practices of people which, over a long period, have assumed the force of law.

cy-près: As near as possible. In testamentary matters, the court will apply the doctrine of *cy-près* to follow the testator's intent as closely as possible.

D

d.s.p.: *demisit-sene-prole*. Died without issue.

damages: An indemnity for loss sought by an injured party through an act or default in contract or tort.

days of grace: Additional days allowed beyond a due date in which to make a payment.

de banco: Of the bench.

de bene esse: Conditionally; in anticipation of future need. An examination *de bene esse* is a pre-trial examination of a witness unable to be at the actual trial.

de bonis non administratis: When an estate has not been wholly settled by the executor an administrator, *de bonis non*, is appointed to handle that part of the estate left incomplete.

de facto: In fact. See **de jure.**

de integro: As it was before; a second time.

de jure: As a matter of law. See **de facto.**

de minimus: A minor matter so that the court will not adjudicate on same.

de novo: Anew; for a second time (*e.g.*, a trial *de novo* is a new trial as ordered by a superior court).

de son tort: Of his own wrong.

debenture: A security for a loan of money issued by a corporation.

D

debt: A sum of money due under an agreement or by way of a court judgment.

declaration: A statement that is unsworn in matters of evidence. Under certain circumstances a court will admit a declaration as evidence.

declatory judgment: A finding or court judgment as to rights of the parties, but no order issuing as to what then must be done.

decree: A judgment and order of the court.

decree absolute: The final decree of the court.

decree nisi: In a divorce action, a decree *nisi* is made in the first instance and not made absolute until after a specified period, often three months.

deed: A written instrument executed and delivered conveying a title or interest in real property.

deem: Something is considered to be.

defamation: The term for words, spoken (slander) or written (libel), tending to injure a person's reputation.

default:'   To omit to do that which by law you are required to do.

defence: The allegations of a defendant in answer to those of the plaintiff.

defendant: The party being sued in court by the plaintiff.

D

degree of proof: The actual amount of proof required to obtain a judgment.

del credere: Guarantee or warranty. An agent who is responsible to a principal for a purchaser's solvency is a *del credere* agent. He undertakes to guarantee the payment of the price for which goods are sold.

delegatus non potest delegare: A delegate cannot delegate; authority cannot be delegated further without a principal's consent.

delicto, action ex: Indicating an action of tort.

delivery: The transfer of possession from one person to another.

demise: To grant a lease on land implying a covenant on the part of the lessor for quiet enjoyment.

demurrer: An admission that a charge against a defendant is true, but of no legal consequence.

deponent: A person who gives evidence by affidavit or orally.

deport: To remove an alien from a country, often due to illegal entry.

depose: To make a statement on oath; to make a deposition.

deposition: A statement under oath, similar to an **affidavit.**

derogate: To evade or to take away from. Derogation from the grant. When one has undertaken to lease land, use of the land cannot be obstructed in a way contrary to terms of the lease.

descendent: A person who is a child, grandchild etc. of the person who has died. See **ascendent.**

D

detinue: An action whereby a plaintiff seeks return of property or its value. An action in tort.

devastavit: A neglect of duty of a personal representative making him personally liable to claims on assets by, for example, creditors and legatees.

deviation: A change or departure from a plan mutually agreed upon.

devise: A written bequest in a will. It refers to real property. See **bequeath**.

dictum: An opinion of a judge. See **obiter dicta**.

die without issue: When a person dies leaving no children at the date of death.

digamy: A second marriage after the death of the first spouse.

direct evidence: Evidence which bears directly on the point at issue. See **circumstantial evidence.**

direction to a jury: Instructions given to a jury by a judge to clarify a point of law enabling the jury to properly apply the law to the facts in the case.

director: A person who conducts the affairs of a corporation.

disbar: The process of depriving a lawyer of status in the legal profession.

discharge: Generally meaning to relieve of an obligation or responsibility.

disclaimer: A denial, refusal or renunciation of an act.

D

discount: An allowance deducted from an amount payable; an allowance made for advancing money upon bills before due date.

discovery: Facts under oath. See **examination for discovery**.

dishonor: Wherein a drawee of a bill of exchange refuses to accept or pay it.

dismissal of action: An action of a judge in rejecting the plaintiff's case. An end to the particular proceedings as for lack of jurisdiction. Another suit may be brought at a later date if the first is dismissed without prejudice.

disorderly house: A brothel.

dissenting opinion: A finding of a judge explaining his views as opposed to majority opinion.

dissolution: The act of breaking up, or ending (*e.g.*, a partnership, marriage, corporation, etc.).

distrain: To seize goods by distress.

distress: The seizing of a personal chattel in satisfaction of a wrong committed. Commonly refers to a landlord seizing goods for non-payment of rent.

distribution: The division of an estate of an intestate among the next of kin.

District Attorney: The public prosecutor of the U.S. government in each of the federal judicial districts. Also, under state governments, the prosecutor representing the state in each of its judicial districts. Must be a lawyer and elected by the people. Sometimes called State's Attorney. See **Crown prosecutor**; **prosecutor**.

D

dividend: Periodic income from an investment in stocks, shares and the like.

divorce: The termination of marriage by law as distinct from ending by death or annulment.

dock: The place in court where a prisoner stands or sits while on trial.

docket number: A number assigned to a case by a court clerk and is used on all pleadings with respect to the case.

domicile: The place of a person's fixed and permanent home. It may be domicile of birth or domicile of choice.

dominant tenement: An estate of land the owner of which enjoys the benefit of an easement over a servient tenement estate (*e.g.*, a right of way).

donatio mortis causa: A gift by reason of death. One must be in imminent danger of death and have delivered personal property to the donee. If the person does not die the property reverts back.

donee: One who receives a gift from another (the donor).

donor: One who makes a gift to another (the donee).

dormant partner: A silent or limited partner. One who contributes money and receives profits but takes no part in the operation of the partnership.

double insurance: Where a person has two contracts for insurance on the same risk. One may only recover an actual loss, not more, as insurance is a contract of indemnity, not one to profit.

D

dower: A wife's right to a life estate interest in one-third of the real property held by her husband in fee simple during their marriage.

dowry: That which a wife brings to her husband in marriage.

draft: A cheque or bill of exchange; a rough copy of a document.

drawee: One who is expected to accept a bill of exchange.

drawer: A person who draws a bill of exchange.

duces tecum: To bring with thee. A subpoena which commands a person to appear in court, and to bring writings, etc., for review by the court.

dum casta vixerit: So long as she shall live chaste. Called a *dum casta* clause at common law and used in a separation agreement, requiring a wife to remain chaste in order to receive her allowance under the agreement.

duress: Where compulsion is threatened and a person acts in fear of personal injury. Contracts made under duress are voidable by the person threatened.

dwelling: A building used as a residence, including the land and outbuildings thereon.

E

e.o.e.:   Errors and omission excepted.

earnest: That which is given as a security to bind a bargain.

easement: A right enjoyed by one owner of real property over the real property of another (*e.g.*, a right of way).

edict: A command or proclamation.

effects: Personal property, goods and chattels.

ejusdem generis: Of the same kind or nature. In interpretation of statutes the rule is if particular clauses are specified by name, the general words following are taken to apply to the class of those specifically mentioned.

eleemosynary institution: Established for perpetual distribution of free alms or bounties to such class of persons as directed (*e.g.*, hospitals, colleges, universities).

emancipation: To free from control of another or others.

embezzlement: Misappropriation of an employer's personal property by an agent or servant.

emblements: The profits of a crop which has been sown (*e.g.*, products created annually by industry, wheat as opposed to grass.

eminent domain: The right of a state to use of property of a citizen for the common good of all citizens.

emptor: A buyer. See **caveat emptor**.

E

enabling statute: A statute that permits persons to do that which, prior to the statute, they could not do.

encroachment: An intrusion or invasion of a thing, such as a fence, into, over, or on public or private property, thereby lessening its value.

encumbrance: A right, or claim, binding land in existence for another, reducing the value of the land (*e.g.*, a lien or mortgage).

endowment: A permanent provision for something (*e.g.*, money for a person or institution).

engrossing: The copying of a legal instrument.

enjoin: A command in equity to someone to do or not do a specific act; *e.g.*, an **injunction**.

enter an appearance: To reply to a writ of summons within the prescribed time or suffer judgment by default.

entrapment: An action by an officer of the law to encourage the commission of a crime by a suspect in a criminal matter.

enure: To take effect or be available. It is used to indicate that something becomes available to the benefit of another.

equitable assets: Assets of a deceased person available to a creditor only through a court sitting in equity.

equity: A concept wherein flexibility is superimposed on an inflexible common law edict (*e.g.*, damages in common law may not be just in a breach of contract to sell a rare antique, whereas specific performance, or a court ordering a person to honor his contract, and perform, is an equitable remedy).

E

equity of redemption: The right of a mortgagor on full payment of a mortgage debt to redeem title on the property free of the loan.

escheat: A reversion to the state of real and personal property when the owner dies intestate and with no legal heir.

escrow: Something held by another, not a party thereto, until a condition is met by the party to be benefited in the matter.

essence of a contract: In contracts, something, such as time, stated to be of the essence. Any such stipulation must be strictly followed.

estate: In real property, the degree, nature or quantity of land a person has. In matters testamentary, all property, real and personal, of the deceased.

estoppel: The law intervenes in some cases and estops, or stops, a person from alleging certain things which then cannot be proved.

et al.: *et alii*. And others.

et seq.: *et sequentes*. And those which follow.

et ux.: *et uxor*. And wife.

eviction: Dispossession of a tenant by a landlord.

evidence: Subject matter presented during litigation to clarify points at issue for one or the other of the litigants.

ex contractu: An action arising from breach of contract.

E

ex curia: Out of court (*e.g.*, the jurisdiction was *ex curia*).

ex gratia: As a matter of grace or favor.

ex officio: By reason of office (*e.g.*, the judge acted *ex officio*).

ex parte: On one side only. A matter of procedure, where *ex parte* application is made with the other party absent.

ex post facto: Something done after the fact of time affecting something else that was done earlier.

examination for discovery: The pre-trial examination and cross-examination under oath of the parties to an action enabling the plaintiff and defendant to more properly assess each other's case. Similarly, discovery of documents or examination of books, ledgers, etc., relevant to the facts at issue.

execution: The signing of written instruments making them legally valid; putting into force a sentence passed by a judge.

executor/executrix: A person named in the will of a deceased person to handle the affairs of the estate on obtaining probate.

exemplary damages: In a tortious matter, acts done with malice are awarded exemplary damages in an amount higher than normal.

expropriation: The right of the state to take private real property for public use with compensation to the owner.

expunge: To remove from the record *e.g.*, of the court.

E

extortion: Unlawful or forceful taking of money from another by threat. See **blackmail**.

extradition: The surrender of a person by one country to another by international agreement.

extrajudicial: An act done or words spoken by a judge outside his jurisdiction. See **obiter dicta**.

eye-witness: One giving evidence of a fact directly from personal observation.

F

f.o.b.: Free on board. A term often inserted in contracts in regard to shipping goods (*e.g.*, f.o.b. point of origin means the costs of shipping start at the place of shipment and are to be borne by the purchaser).

factum: An act or deed.

facultative reinsurance: An arrangement to insure a specific risk on a reinsurance basis. It allows the accepting company to accept or reject it. See **treaty reinsurance**.

fait accompli: An accomplished fact.

false arrest: To stop a person's freedom of movement; to restrain or incarcerate illegally. See **incarceration**.

false imprisonment: To imprison a person without lawful cause. It may refer to a civil action or criminal action.

false pretence: A false statement made to obtain a benefit, chattel or money with the intent to defraud another; theft.

falsify: To prove a thing to be false; to tamper with a document by any means.

fee: Signifies an estate or interest in land.

fee simple: The maximum interest a person can possess in land.

fee tail: An estate in land limited to a person and the heirs of his body.

felo de se: Self murder, or suicide.

F

felony: Crimes involving imprisonment for more than a year. In the U.S.A. a felony is distinguished from a misdemeanor, or a lesser crime. See **indictable offence; misdemeanor; summary conviction.**

feme convert: A married woman.

feme sole: A single woman, divorcee or widow.

ferae naturae: Of a wild nature. Wild animals are so designated from those naturally tame.

feud: See **fee**.

fi. fa.: See **fieri facias.**

fiat: Let it be done. In some litigation a fiat is necessary to proceed with the action.

fiduciary estate: The interest or estate held by a trustee in performance of his duty as a trustee.

fieri facias or fi. fa.: A writ of execution addressed to a sheriff to enforce a judgment of the court.

final judgment: A judgment of the court awarded when an action is closed, as compared to an interlocutory or interim judgment.

fire insurance policy: A contract to insure against loss by fire.

firm: A business partnership.

F

first instance, court of: The court in which an action is first heard, distinct from a court of appeal or court of last resort. See **last resort**.

fitiate: To invalidate or cancel a contract.

fixtures: Something in connection with, or fixed to, real property and things appurtenant thereto.

flagrante delicto, in: While the offense is being committed; caught in the act.

flotsam: Goods which are afloat after a shipwreck. See **jetsam**.

force majeure: Irresistible coercion imposed on someone.

forcible entry: The taking possession of lands or tenements by force. This type of entry is capable of redress in both a civil and criminal action.

foreclosure: The right of a mortgagee to take legal action when the mortgagor defaults in payment under the mortgage.

foreman: The principal and presiding member of a jury.

forensic science: A science which is medical and legal in nature; medical and legal examination and evaluation of a suspected murder.

forgery: The making of a false document intending another to act on it or use it as if genuine. See **uttering**.

forma pauperis: In the form or character of a pauper.

forthwith: In a reasonable time.

F

frauds, statute of: A statute passed to attempt to avoid fraud. It requires any dealing in land to be in writing and to be enforceable by the courts. Likewise, a promise to answer the debt of another or a contract to operate in a period greater than one year must be in writing to be enforced by the courts.

freehold: Land held in fee or for a term of life. Complete ownership of land. See **fee simple.**

from: In law of contract, this word excludes the date of execution.

frustration: In contract law, an impossibility of carrying out the promises made (*e.g.,* the subject-matter of the contract being destroyed and thus non-existent for the purposes of the contract).

functus officio: A person whose authority has ended.

furandi animus: The intention of stealing.

future estate: An estate not to be effective in terms of possession until a later time; a remainder estate in fee simple.

G

garnishee: A person who is garnished or warned to pay a debt to a creditor. The order is referred to as a garnishee order of the court.

garnishment: A warning or notice used in the attachment of debts. See **garnishee**.

gazette: An official publication of a provincial or state government. Notices and advices placed in a gazette as required by law are evidence of the fact and of date of publication.

general lien: In law of bailment, the right of a bailee to hold a chattel until payment is made by the bailor–owner.

gift: A conveyance, or transfer, which passes property in land or personalty.

good consideration: Consideration based on natural true love and affection. Will not sustain an action for breach of contract. This is not valuable consideration in contract law.

good faith: Bona fide. An intent to deal in an honest manner with another.

goodwill: Encompasses all the good and valuable relationships in a business venture. Along with the well-known firm name, goodwill is considered part of the business at the time of sale.

grand jury: A group of persons called to assess the validity of a criminal charge against an accused. If the accusation is found valid the person is formally accused.

grant: A term used in matters of conveyance of land to indicate transfer of the interest from one person to another.

G

grant to uses: Conveyance of realty to a man to avoid dower and its restrictions in jurisdictions where dower applies; a man may sell the land to another without a bar of dower by his wife.

grantee: The buyer, or person, to whom interest in real property is transferred.

grantor: The sellor, or person, transferring an interest in land to the grantee.

gratuitous: A thing done or passed to another without consideration. Free.

guarantee: A promise by one person to answer as surety for the debt or obligation of another.

guardian: One who has the custody and charge of a person or thing (*e.g.*, an infant who lacks capacity in law to manage his own affairs). A guardian may be appointed by power of appointment or by a will. See **conservator**.

guardian ad litem: An infant in judicial proceedings is defended by a guardian *ad litem*.

H

habeas corpus: That you have the body. Established to ensure that no one is kept imprisoned indefinitely without a charge being made.

habendum: The clause in a deed that sets out the estate or interest granted by the deed. See **to have and to hold**.

habitual criminal: An individual who repeatedly commits major crimes. See **recidivist**.

half-blood: A relationship between two persons who have one common ancestor. See **whole blood**.

head note: In reported decisions of the courts, at the beginning thereof, a summary of the issues in question.

hearing: Generally, the trial of an action by the courts.

hearsay evidence: Evidence with respect to facts not seen or heard by the witness, but reported by the witness for another. Such evidence is generally inadmissable.

heir/heiress: One who inherits, by right of blood, realty and personalty.

holder: A payee or endorsee in possession of a bill of exchange or promissory note.

holder in due course: A person who has taken a bill of exchange, or note, complete and regular on its face, who became holder before it was overdue with no notice of earlier dishonour and who took it in good faith and for value with no notice of a defect in the title of the negotiator.

H

holding company: A company created to hold the shares of subsidiaries.

holding out: Persuading others to believe in the existence of an authority one does not have in fact. This person may later be estopped from denying the apparent authority.

holograph: Written entirely in a person's own hand. A holograph will is one written in the testator's own hand and signed by him alone.

homicide: Causing the death of a human being by any means.

honorarium: A gratuity or tip given another for service.

hostile witness: A witness wherein it is evident the witness holds a bias adverse to the party examining him.

human being: The foetus in one view becomes a human being when it has proceeded in a living state from the body of its mother, whether or not it has breathed, has independent circulation, or the unbilical cord is severed. Some maintain a human being exists at conception.

hypothec: Security for a debt that remains in the possession of the debtor (*e.g.,* a mortgage of land where the mortgagee is not in possession).

I

i.o.u.: I owe you. A written acknowledgment of a debt.

ibid.: *Ibidem*. In the same case.

ignorantia juris neminem excusat: Ignorance of the law excuses no man.

immoral contract: A contract based on an immoral reason, (*contra bonos mores*) is void.

immovable: Realty that is tangible but cannot be moved.

in camera: In private. An action may be heard *in camera*, or in chambers to ensure privacy or to distinguish points of law.

in loco parentis: In the place of a parent.

in personam: Against the person; *e.g.*, an action against a person rather than a thing. See **in rem**.

in rem: An action where relief is not desired against a person. These actions are usually for a claim to property or title, to recover land. See **in personam**.

in terrorem: As a threat. May be in reference to a legacy in a will, which is void if threat is proved.

incarceration: To cause a person to be jailed. See **false arrest**.

incorporate: To create a separate legal entity or person recognized by law. This is known as a corporation or limited liability company in some jurisdictions.

I

indemnity: To make good to another, or to indemnify. An insurance contract is one of indemnity, or one to compensate a person at the time of loss.

indenture: A document, deed or contract setting out certain agreements or objects between the parties.

indictable offence: One of the more serious criminal offences (*e.g.*, murder, all sexual crimes, breaking and entering, etc.). See **felony**.

indictment: A formal accusation charging a person with a crime.

inevitable accident: An act of God; something bound to happen. See **vis major**.

infant: An under-age person, 18 to 21 years depending on the jurisdiction, who, legally, has no capacity to undertake a legal obligation.

inferior court: One whose jurisdiction is limited by statute. The amount of money for which you sue determines which court in a civil action has jurisdiction.

information, laying of: In criminal law, a process whereby a person is accused of an offence, causing the launching of a prosecution in law.

infringement: To intrude on another's right. Used specifically in reference to copyright or patent.

injunction: A court order to a person or persons to do or not to do a particular thing.

I

inquest: An inquiry held by a coroner into sudden, violent or unusual death.

insanity: A state of being insane, whereby one cannot understand the nature and results of his or her acts and has no legal capacity.

insolvent: A bankrupt whose assets cannot cover debts.

instrument: A written legal document.

insurable interest: A basic concept in insurance, whereby an individual stands in such a relationship to something that he may lose by its loss. To insure anything one must have such an interest in same.

insurance commissioner: In several states in the U.S.A., a public officer whose duty is to supervise insurance matters as conducted by foreign and domestic companies. See **superintendent of insurance**.

insured: The person who receives an agreement of indemnity from an insurance company.

insurer: An insurance company that agrees to indemnify an insured against certain perils.

inter alia: Amongst other things.

inter vivos: During a lifetime; between living persons.

interest: A title or right to personal or real property; income from an investment of money.

I

interlineation: To write between the lines in a legal document, such as a deed or will. It is not valid unless properly initialed at the time of execution of the instrument.

interlocutory: An interim phase with reference to an action.

interlocutory injunction: An injunction that is granted by the court until a decision is given by the court as to the merit of the case at issue.

interlocutory judgment: An intermediate judgment, given upon some defence and which does not complete the action.

international law: The rights and duties of citizens of different states to one another; the rights and duties of states to one another.

intestate: Without a will. A person dies intestate when he or she dies without leaving a will. The estate descends to the next of kin by statute.

intra vires: Within the power. See **ultra vires**.

inventory: A list compiled in order to apply to the court for probate on administration. It contains all realty and personalty held by the deceased at the date of his death.

invitee: A person on a premises for business purposes. The occupier must use reasonable care to prevent damage to the invitee from any unusual danger which he knows or ought to know exists. See licensee; trespasser.

ipso facto: By the mere fact.

irrevocable: Something that cannot be revoked or cancelled (*e.g.*, a power of appointment or power of attorney).

issue: The children of a marriage; the matter in disagreement between the parties in litigation.

J

jactitation of marriage: To boast or hold that one party is married to another when it is not the case. This can effect an individual's reputation as to matrimony and a court may order the party making the claim to be silent.

jetsam: Goods thrown overboard to lighten a ship which is likely to sink. See **flotsam**.

joinder of parties: The joining together of two or more persons in one action.

joining of action: The process of joining several related causes of action into one action.

joint and several: Partners are liable jointly and severally which means they may be sued alone or together being responsible for the actions of each other.

joint tenancy: A situation in land holding in which two or more persons have an undivided interest in land with equal right to possession and equal title. It is acquired through the same conveyance and all enjoy a right of survivorship on the death of the other. See **unity of possession**.

judge-advocate-general: An officer appointed to advise the government with regard to court-martial and military law.

judgment: An order of the court in a civil matter; the sentence of a court in a criminal matter.

judgment creditor: A person who has received judgment in his favour and is thus entitled to enforce an execution to obtain restitution under the judgment.

J

judicial notice: A court may take notice of a state of affairs and formal proof is not needed.

judicial separation: In some jurisdictions, a separation of man and wife by a court. In others, a separation agreement is a matter of contract between the parties not a determination of a court.

jurat: A statement at the end of an affidavit indicating where, when and before whom it was sworn.

juridical: Acting in the administration of justice. The days a court sits in administration of justice are juridical days.

jurisdiction: The power vested in a court by the legislature to hear and decide on different types of cases.

jurisprudence: The study or the science of law.

juror: A member of a duly constituted jury.

jury: A group of men or women, peers of the accused, chosen and called to hear and decide on fact in matters before the court, both criminal or civil.

jury trial: A trial before a jury who must make a decision on the facts of the case.

jus: Law or right.

jus gentium: The law of nations.

jus in personam: A right against a specific person.

jus in rem: A right against all the world, not just a person.

J

jus tertii: The right of a third party. This does not apply in case of an agent against a principal.

justices of assize: Judges of superior courts sent to various areas to preside at court sittings.

justification: The showing of an adequate reason why a defendant did what he is charged with.

juvenile (no publicity): When a child under the age of sixteen is to be tried in court it must take place without publicity.

juvenile courts: The courts having jurisdiction with regard to children under sixteen years of age in matters of domestic strife; family court.

juvenile offender: A juvenile who has been charged with an indictable offence. The family court judge may refer the case to adult court if it would be of benefit to the accused and to the public in some jurisdictions.

K

K.B.: The Court of the King's Bench (in Canada and England).

K.C.: King's Counsel (in Canada and England).

keeping the peace: A court may order a person to keep the peace and be of good behavior for a specific reason and time.

kidnapping: The taking away, or abduction, of any person against his will. Usually for purposes of ransom, or extortion.

kin: Kindred. Legal relationship, usually by blood lines rather than by marriage.

kind, in: Payment in kind is payment made in services or property rather than money.

King's evidence: The practice of giving evidence for the Crown hoping for a lighter sentence or pardon. See **State's evidence**.

kleptomania: An irresistable desire to steal.

L

laches: Neglect in asserting one's rights in law to the point where the rights are barred. See **limitation of action**.

land: A general term referring to real property and all buildings and things fixed thereto.

land registration: A system of land registration in order to establish legally who the rightful owner of real property is, and the encumbrances thereon.

land tax: Any system used by federal, provincial, state, or municipal authority to raise tax revenues from land for the common good.

landlord: A person who holds title or property in realty and leases possession to another person known as a tenant.

lapse: In contract law, an offer ceasing in a reasonable time if no specific time is stated; in estate law, the failure of a disposition by will where the intended beneficiary predeceases the testator.

larceny: In the U.S.A., a technical name for theft. Petty larceny is theft of small amounts, set by statute, usually under $50.00. Above that amount, it is known as grand larceny. Petty larceny is a misdemeanor and grand larceny is a felony. The term has been abolished in Canada and the U.K.

last clear chance: A doctrine in tort law giving judgment to the plaintiff, even if he or she has contributed to negligence, if the defendant could have avoided an accident by use of reasonable care.

last resort: The Supreme Court of a country from which no further appeal is possible. See **first instance, court of.**

L

law society: A society of lawyers exercising control over its members, dealing with misconduct and holding the right to disbar a member guilty of conduct unbecoming of the profession.

lawyer: A person permitted to practice law and to give legal advice. See **attorney; barrister; counsel; solicitor.**

lay: Denoting a non-professional person.

leading cases: Cases in law which establish a pattern to follow in future cases; precedent.

leading question: A question which by the way it is phrased implies or suggests the answer sought. In rules of evidence, they are not allowed in direct examination, but are allowed in cross-examination.

lease: A method of establishing a right for use and possession of land but not ownership. The lessor owns the land, the lessee rents and uses it by verbal or written agreement. Personal property may also be leased.

leasehold: An interest in land, but not one of freehold. See **lease**.

legacy: A bequest or a gift made to another under the terms of a will.

legal aid: A system whereby persons have access to legal aid with payment determined by their financial income and which ensures that all people are represented by a lawyer.

legal description: A clear and definite description by which property may be located and identified.

L

legal tender: Tender offered in payment of a debt and recognized as legal money.

legitimation (per subsequens matrimonium): The legitimation of children by the subsequent marriage of their parents.

lessee: The person who holds a lease giving possession or use of lands.

lessor: The person who leases to another while retaining legal ownership.

letters of administration: A document issued by a court appointing someone to administer the estate of an intestate.

letters patent: In letters patent jurisdictions, governmental authority to form a corporation (*e.g.*, the medium creating the legal entity).

lex domicilii: The law of the place of a person's domicile. See **domicile**.

lex fori: The law of the forum (the place where a case is heard).

lex loci contractus: The law of the place where a contract is made.

lex talionus: Law of the jungle; law based on an idea of an eye for an eye.

liability: An obligation imposed by law on a person by common law, equity or statute.

L

libel: A written defamatory comment on a person's character. See **defamation; slander**.

licence: Authority given to a person to do something that, lacking such authority, would be unlawful.

licensee: A person entering a premises gratuitously. The occupier must warn the person of any concealed dangers or become liable for any injury. See **invitee**.

lie: If a cause of action is legally sound it is said to lie.

lien: A legal right whereby a creditor may cause a debtor's property to be sold and the monies received applied to payment of the debts. See **mechanic's lien**.

limitation of action: The concept of barring a person's right of action after a time set by statute and reckoned from the date on which the cause of action arose. See **laches**.

limitation of liability: In corporation law, the limit placed on a shareholder's liability for acts done by the corporation.

limited partnership: A partnership having general partners, and limited, sleeping or silent, partners. The latter contribute money to the firm but do not participate in its operation. They are entitled to profits but are not liable for obligations of the partnership beyond the sum they have contributed.

liquidated damages: A genuine pre-estimate by parties to a contract to establish an amount to be paid the other for an anticipated breach of contract.

liquidator: A person appointed to wind up a company's business. See **bankruptcy**.

L

lis pendens: A pending lawsuit, regarding land in particular. The lis pendens may be registered on title until the issue is settled by the courts.

litigant: One of the parties involved in a law suit.

litigation: The process of being involved in a law suit; the court action itself.

litigious: That which is the subject of the court action; the essence of litigation.

local courts: Courts with a geographical limit in jurisdiction, such as district, county and police courts.

loco parentis, in: In the place of a parent.

locus in quo: The place where it is alleged something has been done.

lodger: A person having use and possession of part of a house.

lottery: A game of chance which does not involve choice or skill; the distribution of money or prizes by chance.

lucid interval: Sanity occurring between attacks of insanity. A contract made by a lucid person is valid.

lynch law: Law executed by a mob without regard for the processes of law available in a jurisdiction.

M

maintenance: Payments made after a marriage has been dissolved or during separation. Often synonymous with alimony.

majority: Adult age, 18 to 21, depending on the jurisdiction, at which time one has capacity to act for oneself.

mala fides: Bad faith.

mala in se: Moral offences that go against the conscience.

malice: Wicked purpose.

malicious prosecution: A prosecution commenced without reasonable or probable cause.

malinger: To pretend to be sick or disabled to avoid a duty. Has particular reference to the armed forces.

mandamus: A superior court order to an inferior court requiring it to do a particular thing.

manifest: A document signed by a shipper describing goods carried.

manslaughter: Unlawful killing of another without intent.

marital: The nature of marriage and interaction therein.

marriage: The legal ceremony establishing the relationship of husband and wife.

marriage settlement: A written agreement settling questions of property, made between a man and woman prior to their marriage.

M

maturity: Bills and notes are mature when the due date arrives; age of maturity. See **majority**.

measure of damage: The criteria used by a court to determine the amount of damage to be given in a case.

mechanic's lien: An instrument that may be registered against land to establish claim by a worker for wages, a contractor for costs or a supplier of materials for payment.

meeting of minds: Where the parties to a contract are in complete agreement to all terms of the contract. See **consensus ad idem**.

memorandum of association: A document filed by persons with which to form an incorporated company. See **letters patent**.

mens rea: Mental intent or guilt of mind essential in most serious offences (*e.g.*, murder).

mensa et thoro: From bed and board.

merits: A court will consider a case on its merits; the main issue in the action.

metes and bounds: Land description with boundary lines set by angles and end points. Bounds refer to the boundary lines and metes to a limiting mark.

midwife: A woman who assists others at childbirth.

minor: A person under legal age, 18 to 21 depending on the jurisdiction.

minutes: A record kept of a meeting.

M

miscarriage: A failure of justice. Appeals lie where there has been a substantial miscarriage of justice.

misdemeanor: A crime involving a fine or imprisonment for less than a year. See **felony; indictable offence; summary conviction offence**.

misrepresentation: By words or conduct, to make a false statement of fact.

mistrial: An erroneous trial due to a technicality.

mitigation: A lessening of damages; a lessening of a penalty in a criminal action.

moiety: Half.

moot: A point that is debatable. Moot court is a setting for students to practice and learn court procedures.

moral turpitude: An act of a person which offends the moral standards of society.

more or less: In property description, a term to allow for slight inaccuracies, with both parties ready to assume any risk arising because of same.

mortgage: A duly executed instrument in writing that becomes a lien on real property. It is security for payment of a specified debt.

mortgagee: A party who takes a mortgage to be sure of payment of money he has loaned the mortgagor.

M

mortgagor: A party who pledges property as a security for a loan.

mortuary: A funeral home; a place for the preparation of human remains for the purpose of burial or cremation.

motion: An application to a court for a ruling or order.

municipal law: The by-laws and ordinances of a municipality.

murder, capital: Murder where capital punishment (or death) is the penalty enforced on a convicted accused.

murder, first degree: In Canada, when convicted of premeditated murder, a mandatory term of 25 years in prison is imposed. In the U.S.A., a deliberate and premeditated murder may be subject to capital punishment.

murder, second degree: In Canada and the U.S.A., unintentional murder without premeditation. See **manslaughter.**

mutatis mutandis: To include whatever changes of a minor nature are needed.

mutiny: Where two or more persons attempt to overthrow lawful authority in the armed services.

N

name: The surname (last) or the christian (first) name of a person.

narcotic: A substance defined by statute in various jurisdictions which in moderate doses relieves pain but in excess may cause an individual to develop a desire or need to continue to take the substance (*e.g.*, opium, morphine, etc.).

nations, law of: See **jus gentium**.

natural affection: Used as consideration in contracts between relatives.

natural child (natural born): The child born of a woman, legitimate or illegitimate, as compared to an adopted child.

naturalization: To give a foreigner the status of a natural-born citizen.

natural law: Law of nature, law arising from reason.

necessaries: In reference to an infant, necessaries are food, clothing, shelter, medical help and education. Depending on the condition of life and needs at a given time one may be bound to provide such necessaries by a contract.

necessity: Agent of necessity; whereby a person acts on his best judgment dependent on the emergency of the moment.

negligence: A breach of a duty owed another.

negotiable instruments: Legal instruments purporting to represent a given sum of money (*e.g.*, cheques, bills of exchange, etc.).

N

negotiate: To transfer for value a negotiable instrument.

nemine contradicente (nem. con.):   No one contradicting, or dissenting, in voting on a matter; unanimously.

nepos: Grandson.

neptis: Granddaughter.

new trial: Will be ordered in case of misdirection by a judge to a jury.

newly-born child: A person under the age of one year.

next friend: An adult person acting for an infant who lacks the capacity to act for himself in a legal proceeding.

next of kin: A person related in close degree to another person.

nihil: Nothing. It is possible a writ of execution will return nihil.

nolens volens: Whether willing or unwilling.

nolo contendere: I will not contest it. In a criminal action, the defendant states he will not defend himself. It is virtually a plea of guilty and judgment may go against him at the court's discretion.

nolle prosequi: To be unwilling to prosecute. In effect, a plaintiff withdraws a claim against a defendant.

nominal damages: A small sum received by a plaintiff who has won a case indicating the jury feels the plaintiff has not suffered substantial damage.

N

non compos mentis: Not of sound mind. Refers to persons with mental imbalance.

non est factum: To deny that an instrument or deed was executed by the one who so denies.

non-sequitur: It does not follow. Used in an argument to claim an inference drawn is incorrect.

notice: A notification of fact.

notice d.o.r.: In proceedings of foreclosure a mortgagor files notice in court that he desires an opportunity to redeem.

novation: To replace the old with new (*e.g.*, an obligation or debtor).

novus actus interveniens: A new act intervening.

nudum pactum: A nude contract or bare promise with no consideration.

nuisance: Something that unlawfully damages another.

nulla bona: No goods.

nullius filius: The son of no man; a bastard.

nunc pro tunc: Now instead of then. To enter a document so as to have the same legal effect as if it had been entered earlier.

nuptials: The celebration of marriage in accordance with law.

O

oath: A requirement that a statement be made by a party before God to witness all statements as true. A person with no religious beliefs may affirm as to the truth of the statement.

oath of allegiance: An oath to bear true allegiance to the state. Used in naturalization proceedings.

obiter dicta: *Ex gratia* statements by a judge in, but not necessary for, judgment. Does not become binding as a precedent. See **ratio decidendi**.

objection: A procedure during a trial where evidence is questioned as to its validity or admissibility.

obligation: A duty that is legal or moral and not in the nature of physical compulsion.

occurrence: In insurance contracts, coverage is on an occurrence or accident basis. In the former case it must just happen, in the latter case it must arise by accident.

offer: A proposal or offer to do something. If accepted by another, it is a contract. It may be cancelled, changed or revoked anytime prior to acceptance or within a reasonable time.

offer and acceptance: One party, the offeree, must signify assent to a proposal of the offeror to bind the parties to a contract.

offeree: A party to a contract who signifies assent to a proposal, or offer, of the offeror.

offeror: The party to a contract who offers a proposal for acceptance by the offeree.

O

officer: A principal member of a corporation such as the President, Treasurer, Controller, etc.

ombudsman: An individual who investigates decisions, recommendations, and commissions and acts in the administration of governments. Supervisory power over the administration of justice is not included in the powers of his office.

onus probandi: The burden of proof. Usually resting on the plaintiff who alleges the defendant damaged him in some way.

open policy: In insurance, a contract where the value of property insured must be proved after loss. In a valued policy, the value is fixed when the contract is made.

option: In real property, an offer that is kept open for another for a specified time.

oral pleadings: Pleadings in court *viva voce* (orally).

order: A court act that does not decide the case on its merits but directs something to be done or not done, an interlocutory injunction being issued until the merits are decided.

ordinary life: In insurance, also known as straight or whole life. The insured pays premiums as long as he lives, his estate is paid the face value of the policy at his death.

out of court: The situation where before trial commences a settlement is made by private agreement, usually on new evidence being found.

over: In conveyancing, a gift over means a gift will come into being on a particular estate being determined.

O

over insurance: Insurance in several policies in an amount greater than the value of the item insured.

over-riding: In insurance, an agent may get an over-riding, extra commission, to cover unusual expenses.

overt act: An open, non-secretive act.

owner: The person who has title to real or personal property.

ownership: Exclusive right to use and possess something real or personal.

P

pari passu: In proportion or equal footing. Creditors of an insolvent share in proportion to their claims.

parol: Verbal; by word of mouth; not written.

parol contract: A verbal contract.

parol evidence: Evidence given verbally to the court. In law of contract, the written word supercedes a verbal statement with respect to the contract.

parole: To release a person from prison subject to certain conditions and penalty of return should he default; to report to a probation officer regularly. See **probation**.

partial loss: In insurance, where insurance is not exhausted after loss.

particular estate: In real property, an estate in a grantee prior to a reversion or remainder. See **remainder; reversion**.

parties (to an action):   The plaintiff and defendant in a court case.

partition: To divide an estate held in joint tenancy so that each party holds an undivided share.

partnership: Persons who enter a business relationship with a view to making a profit.

party-wall: A dividing wall between two properties which each adjacent owner may use.

P

patent: Authority from the government for a first inventor of something to have exclusive benefit from it for a certain period, usually seventeen years.

patricide (parricide): The murder of one's father.

pawn: To hand over a chattel as security for a debt; a pledge.

payee: The person to whom money is paid.

payer: The person who pays the payee.

payment into court: To deposit money in the court registry pending the outcome of litigation.

peaceful enjoyment: The right of a person in law to the use and possession of his property whether rented or owned. See **quiet enjoyment**.

pecuniary: Referring to money; *e.g.*, to suffer pecuniary loss or enjoy pecuniary gain.

peer: An equal. A jury is comprised of a group of the defendant's peers.

penal laws: Laws imposing penalties for doing a prohibited act.

penalty: Punishment in terms of a pecuniary fine.

pendente lite: While a suit is pending, or after it has commenced. In estate law, administration is granted *pendente lite* if a will's validity is questioned in court.

per autre vie: For another's life.

P

per capita: Distribution by head count.

per curiam: By the court.

per quod: By reason of which.

per se: In or of itself.

per stirpes: See **stirpes, distribution per**.

peremptory: A final or determinate act.

peremptory challenge: A request to the court to dismiss a prospective juror.

performance: To do a thing agreed upon.

performance bond: An insurance bond guaranteeing performance of a contract. It does not cover labor and material costs.

peril: The cause of a loss. In insurance, it may be fire, theft, or vandalism.

perjury: Wilfully making an untrue, or false, statement in a judicial proceeding.

permit: A license to do something lawful.

perpetuity: In estate law, a settlement cannot be made in perpetuity, beyond a life or lives in being, at death of the donor plus twenty-one years. *Cy-près* may, on occasion, be resorted to by the court. See **cy-près**.

person: Any human being or legally constituted corporation.

P

personal action: An action brought by an injured party on his own behalf.

personal property: Things clearly not real property and which are movable and tangible chattels.

personal property floater: A broad coverage insurance contract, virtually all risks are covered.

petition: Generally, any pleading, or appeal, to a court for relief (*e.g.*, a petition for divorce or a petition for relief in bankruptcy).

petty jury: Twelve persons impanelled for trial of issues of fact.

picketing: The practice of walking or parading before a place of business to make public a labor grievance. To picket peacefully is lawful.

pilfer: To take, steal, small articles.

plaintiff: The party commencing a suit in court against the defendant.

pleading: The drawing of written pleadings in an action, or verbally promoting the cause of the party in court.

pledge: The transfer of a chattel to secure repayment of a debt. See **pawn**.

p.m.: *Post meridiam*, or afternoon.

police: A force of persons responsible for maintaining law and order.

P

policy of insurance: A contract.

polyandry: To have more than one living husband at a time.

polygamy: To have more than one living wife at a time.

polygraph: A medical device to record changes in heartbeat, blood pressure, respiration, etc., patterns of which can be used as a lie detector.

possession: To exercise a right of ownership by showing an intent to use.

post: After.

post mortem: After death. A medical examination to ascertain the cause of death.

post-date: Affix a later date. To post-date an instrument means to date it so as to be effective after the actual date of execution.

posthumous child: A child born after the death of its father.

power of attorney: An authorization in writing given by one person to another to act for the former on a specific matter or in general.

power of sale: A clause in a mortgage whereby the mortgagee may on default of payment of the debt advertise and sell the mortgaged property to satisfy the debt.

praecipe: An instrument that directs the issuance of a writ or one containing the particulars of a writ filed in the office from whence the writ will issue.

P

prayer for relief: That part of the pleadings to the court requesting that the defendant be ordered to perform certain acts.

preamble: In statute law, the preamble appears at the beginning of the statute and explains in general terms the purpose of the act.

precatory trust: Found in some wills, a hopeful indication that a thing be done. Such words may perform a binding trust depending on how they are phrased, but generally they just express a wish.

precedents: A case or example that may be followed by the court. The precedent of a higher court binds a lower court in similar cases.

precinct: A boundary, usually geographical, which refers to a particular district over which a police station operates.

prefer: To bring before a court or to lay a charge.

preference shares: In some jurisdictions, known as special shares. They entitle shareholders to a dividend before ordinary or common shareholders receive anything.

prejudice: Often used between lawyers in phrase "without prejudice" to assure that no correspondence may be taken as admitting liability.

preliminary hearing: A pre-trial hearing to determine if there is sufficient cause to hold an accused for actual trial.

premises: The first part of a deed setting out the names involved, the reasons for the deed and the consideration; land granted and any specific building on it.

P

premium: A payment as agreed on for life or property insurance.

prerogative writ: A writ arising from extraordinary powers of the court. See **certiorari; mandamus; prohibition.**

prescription: In land use, a person obtains a prescriptive right to land after twenty years' uninterrupted use in most jurisdictions. It vests property in the user. See **adverse possession**.

presents: A word in a deed, meaning the deed itself.

presumption: An inference to the existence of a fact not known with certainty but rather concluded from the existence of another fact.

presumption of survivorship: In estate matters, if two persons die together, the younger of the two is presumed to have survived the longest.

prima facia: At first glance; on the face of it. *Prima facia* evidence is evidence sufficient to raise a probable case.

primary evidence: The best evidence obtainable.

principal: The interest paid on money borrowed or invested; an individual who employs an agent.

private carrier: A shipper who offers services of carriage for one company only and does not offer same to the general public. See **public carrier**.

private corporation: A company, with membership limited to fifty, which does not offer its shares to the public; a non-offering company.

P

privileged communications: Communications which cannot be disclosed in evidence, such as confidences between solicitor and client.

privity of contract: A direct contractual relationship between parties to the exclusion of all others not party to the contract.

privy: A person who has a direct interest in a thing or cause of action. See **privity of contract**.

pro forma: For form's sake.

pro rata: In proportion or proportionately (*e.g.*, to settle an estate *pro rata* among next of kin).

pro tanto: For as far as it will go, or for so much.

probate: Proving of wills in the appropriate court. Under the seal of the court the executor has the authority to proceed with administration of the estate. It is in common or solemn form. See **common form probate; solemn form probate**.

probation: In lieu of a sentence, a court may order an offender to report regularly to a probation officer for supervision for a certain length of time. Should the offender fail to report or act properly the court may then sentence him to prison.

process: Legal process refers to the writs and documents issued in the commencement and procedure of an action.

procuration (per procurationem):   By means of an agent. Words of procuration on a bill of exchange imply limited authority to sign and puts an acceptor on notice to inquire as to the extent of the authority of the agent; pimping, to procure a person for illegal intercourse.

P

profit à prendre: The right to profit from land. A landowner may lease a farm to another who thus is entitled to harvest the crops and sell them at a profit.

prohibition: A superior court order to stop an inferior court from proceeding in an action. See **certiorari; mandamus; prerogative writ.**

promise: An undertaking by one person to another for performance or non-performance of a thing.

promissory note: An unconditional promise in writing by one person to another, signed by the maker, agreeing to pay on demand or by a fixed time a certain sum of money to a particular person or bearer.

proof of loss: In insurance, a statement or oath made to an insurer to establish the basis of an insured's claim under the insurance contract.

property: Unrestricted and exclusive right to a thing; ownership or title as compared to possession; personal or real property.

property damage: In insurance, damage to physical property of others as compared to personal injury.

property damage (mitigation of): At time of loss an insured is required by law to do all he reasonably can to protect the damaged property from further loss, to mitigate or minimize loss. An insurer is not liable for excess loss should the insured not attempt to so minimize.

prosecution: The proceeding with a legal action; the individual who commences criminal proceedings.

P

prosecutor: One who starts and follows through in a proceeding in the courts. In familiar terms it refers to the Crown (prosecutor) in criminal actions. See **District Attorney.**

prostitution: The selling of one person to another for sexual purposes.

protest: A formal notarized declaration by the holder of a bill of exchange which has been refused payment. The holder declares that he shall pursue the matter and intends to recover all his expenses in pursuit of his rights.

prove: To establish an allegation by means of evidence.

proving a will: To secure formal probate of a will. See **probate**.

proviso: A condition in a deed, its execution as outlined is a prerequisite to the deed's validity.

proximate cause: An action producing an event which never could happen at all without such action.

proxy: In corporate law, a person with authority in writing to vote in place of another; the instrument of proxy itself.

puberty: Age fourteen in males and twelve in females.

public carrier: A shipper or transport company offering services of carriage of goods to the public at large. See **private carrier**.

P

public trustee: An individual appointed by the government to oversee trust situations for persons lacking legal capacity to do so on their own.

publish or publication: In an action for defamation of character, the communication of the defamatory statement to anyone other than the one defamed.

punitive damages: An amount in excess of compensatory damages. Purpose is to make an example of the defendant to others who might so behave.

putative (father): Most commonly used in affiliation proceedings with regard to whom is the alleged father of a child.

Q

Q.B.: The Court of Queen's Bench (in Canada and England).

Q.C.: Queen's Counsel (In Canada and England).

qualified indorsement: On a bill of exchange or promissory note, changing the liability of the indorser from the norm.

quantum meruit: How much he has deserved. An amount that should be paid for service performed as merited.

quash: Annul or make void (*e.g.*, a judgment by an inferior court is quashed by a superior court).

quasi: Meaning as if or almost. See **quasi contract**.

quasi-contract: Where an obligation is assumed by a person as if from a formal contract.

Queen's Bench Court: A superior trial court in some provinces of Canada; Supreme Court of the Province.

quid pro quo: To give a thing of value for something else of like value.

quiet enjoyment: Uninterrupted use and possession. A lessee of a rented house is entitled to quiet enjoyment. See **peaceful enjoyment**.

quit claim deed: A deed of conveyance acting as a release. It passes whatever interest, title or claim a grantor may have. It does not assert validity of title.

quo warranto: A judicial writ commencing an inquiry as to by what authority something was done.

quorum: The minimum number of persons needing to be present at a business meeting to give validity to the decisions of the meeting.

R

R.: Rex or Regina. Used in the report of a criminal case (*e.g., R. v. Jones*) to indicate a suit by the Crown on behalf of the people of Canada against an accused.

ransom: A sum demanded for the release of a person taken prisoner.

rape: Aggravated sexual assault.

rate: In the assessment of property, that part of the value paid as a tax or interest.

ratification: The validation or confirmation of something (*e.g.,* a contract or transaction).

ratio decidendi: The actual reason for a court's decision as compared to *obiter dicta*. See **obiter dicta.**

real: A word used in relation to land or interest in land; real property.

real chattels: Personal chattels or personalty.

real estate broker: One who represents vendors or purchasers of real property for a commission.

realty: The freehold interest in land including things fixed to the land; real estate.

reasonable act: The act of a person which under the circumstances of the case would be considered an ordinary act, or one which a peer would perform in a like case.

R

receiver: One who receives stolen goods, aware that they are stolen; in bankruptcy, a person appointed to receive and deal with a person's property on an interim basis.

recidivist: An habitual criminal; one who repeatedly commits crimes. See **habitual criminal.**

reciprocal contract: One where the consideration is promises that are mutual.

reciprocal will: A will, made by two or more persons making mutual testamentary provisions. Often executed by husband and wife, leaving all property to each other; mutual will.

recital: In a deed, that part setting out matters of fact explaining the reason for the deed.

recission: A court judgment to terminate a contract.

recognizance: An obligation for an accused to appear for trial at the time and place set. See **bail bond.**

reconciliation: Where two parties who have had differences resume normal relations; in separation, a husband and wife may be reconciled and resume cohabitation.

recourse: To resort for payment to those who are secondarily liable on a negotiable instrument.

recovery: To obtain judgment in damages from the court.

rectification: To correct or amend a written instrument to set out the actual intent of the parties.

redemption: The right of a mortgagor to purchase back a mortgaged estate upon full payment of monies due under the mortgage.

R

reductio ad absurdum: Reduction to an absurdity. A method used to prove the error in an argument by showing it leads to an absurd conclusion.

redundancy: Something introduced into a pleading, not needed to establish a cause of action or defence.

re-entry: The right to resume possession of land in a deed or lease on the occasion of a breach of condition by the grantee or lessee.

reeve: The head of a town council or village; mayor.

re-examination: Examination of a witness in reference to matters arising out of cross-examination.

referee: A person selected by parties in dispute to arbitrate their problem.

reference: The referring of a matter to an arbitrator.

reformatory: A prison school with emphasis on rehabilitation and education of young offenders.

regicide: The killing of a king.

register: A record of titles to land; a register of shareholders in a company.

regulation: A rule of an administrative body.

rehearing: An appeal to an appeal court where fresh evidence may be presented.

R

reinsurance: Placing a part of an insurance risk with other insurance companies.

rejoinder: A defendant's answer to a plaintiff's reply. See **pleading**.

relation: A person who is in a blood line with others or a relation by marriage.

release: To surrender a claim against another; a conveyance by a person who has an interest in land, but not possession, whereby rights are given up to the benefit of the person in possession.

relevant: A concept of logic to establish a relationship between two facts, each of which causes the other to be probable.

remainder: Where an estate or interest in land flows out of a greater interest. A remainder vests to the person entitled as soon as the original estate is terminated (*e.g.*, to A for life, remainder to B in fee simple). See **particular estate; reversion**.

remand: To recommit a person to prison; to adjourn a hearing of a criminal charge.

remedial: Statutes which attempt to give a new remedy to rights now in existence.

remedy: A legal means by which to obtain a right or compensation.

remission: The pardon of an offence.

R

remittitur damna: An entry in the record of litigation whereby a plaintiff releases all or part of the damages awarded by a jury. This applies where a jury gives greater damages than the amount claimed.

removal of action: To remove an action from one court to another; to change venue. See **venue**.

render: To restore, or to give up a thing again.

renouncing probate: Where one who has been appointed executor under a will declines the office.

rent: Compensation paid to a landlord by a tenant for the right to use and possess land during the period of the lease.

renunciation, right of: The act of waiving one's rights in estate matters.

repeal: The process of revoking all or part of one statute by another.

replevin: A right to recover things unlawfully taken away which a plaintiff alleges he has an immediate right to possess.

reply: A statement of the plaintiff in answer to an allegation of the defence.

reports: Law reports or histories of litigation with a record of the judge's decision.

representation: A statement or an allegation. See **misrepresentation**.

R

reprieve: The suspension of an order of execution in a criminal sentence.

reprisal: To take something from a wrongdoer to compensate for the wrong done to you; to strike back.

repudiate: To reject or disclaim in order to avoid being liable by implication.

reputation: The good name of a person. See **slander**.

requisitions on title: A letter from the lawyer of a purchaser to the lawyer of the vendor of land with respect to an apparent defect in title requesting its removal therefrom. See **cloud on title.**

res gestae: A fact in criminal law that is directly relevant to the issue, as opposed to hearsay.

res ipsa loquitur: The thing speaks for itself. An allegation in tort that an injury caused by the negligence of another in itself needs no further proof than the fact that the accident happened.

res judicata: That which has already been decided by the court.

res nullius: A thing that has no owner.

rescission: The revocation or cancellation of a contract.

residuary devisee: A person entitled to the balance of a testator's estate in land. See **devise**.

residuary legatee: One who is entitled to share in the balance of a person's personalty after debts and specific bequests have been met under terms of the will.

R

residue: That portion of a person's estate not specifically distributed; the balance of the estate.

resolution: A matter resolved and passed by a majority of shareholders in reference to routine matters of a company. In bankruptcy, a decision by a majority of creditors with respect to these matters is necessary.

respondeat superior: Let the superior be responsible. A principal is liable for acts of an agent, a master for those of a servant, when each is operating in the course of duty.

respondent: The party opposite to a petitioner who must reply to a petition (*e.g.*, in divorce); the defendant in an appeal.

restitutio in integrum: To restore parties in a contract to their original position on its rescission. See **rescission**.

restitution: To return that which has unlawfully been taken away from a person.

restraint of marriage: In estate law, a bequest that is made to restrain a party from marriage is void as it is against public policy.

restraint of trade: Contracts in general restraint are void if unlimited in scope. If in partial restraint they may be valid.

restriction: A limitation placed on the use of property found in a written instrument or deed.

reversible error: An error during trial so serious that a new trial may be required to remedy the error.

reversion: A balance of an estate. The right of the grantors to possession after a particular estate has been fulfilled.

R

right: The interest a person has in real or personal property.

right of action: The right to start a legal action against another.

right of survivorship: On the death of any joint owner in joint tenancy, interest in real property passes to the survivor rather than to the estate.

right of way: The right of a person to pass over another's land.

right to begin: The right of counsel on whom the burden of proof rests to begin addressing the court, presenting arguments and reasoning to satisfy that burden.

riot: The disturbance of public peace by an unlawful assembly of three or more persons in the execution of an unlawful common purpose.

riparian rights: The rights of an owner of land on the banks of watercourses relating to the use of the water on, under and adjacent to the land.

risk: The uncertainty of possible loss in insurance; the personalty insured.

robbery: To steal from another using violence or threat of violence.

roll of the court: A document setting out the business of the court.

root of title: The document with which the abstract of title commences establishing an absolute ownership in land in a registered owner or vendor.

R

royalty: Payments to those so entitled in patents and copyright.

rule: A regulation to govern persons made with their agreement; an order of the court to regulate practice and procedures.

rule of law: The belief that all people are equal before the law.

run with the land: A covenant runs with the land when it goes beyond the original persons in an agreement. All subsequent owners of the land are bound by liabilities or rights in the existing covenants on taking the land.

running down clause: A clause in marine insurance to indicate collision between ships.

S

s.: Used in statute law to refer to a section of an act.

s.p.: *Sine prole*; without issue.

sadism: Sexual gratification achieved by inflicting pain on another.

safe burglary insurance: Specific insurance protection against loss arising from forced entry into a safe or strongbox.

safe conduct: Authority granted by a government to a citizen of a nation at war with that government to freely leave the country.

sale: Transfer of ownership of property from the vendor to the purchaser in consideration of a sum of money.

sale of goods: A contract for the sale of goods in which the seller agrees to transfer the property to the buyer for a monetary consideration.

salvage: Compensation given to people whose voluntary assistance saved a ship, cargo, passengers, or crew from loss or danger at sea; the process of removal of goods during a fire to prevent further damage.

sanction: A penalty provided to enforce obedience to a law.

sans frais: To incur no expense.

sans recours: Without recourse. If an agent signs *sans recours* on a bill of exchange he is not personally liable as he is signing for a principal.

S

satisfaction: The act of satisfying; ending an obligation.

scandal: An allegation whereby a person is demeaned in the public view.

scienter: Claiming in an action that a thing was done knowingly by the defendant.

scilicet: Part of pleadings or affidavits using the words "namely" or "to wit".

script: A draft of a will or codicil or the written instructions for the same.

scrutiny: An examination to check the validity of the votes in an election.

se defendendo: In self defence. Used as a plea in defence of a charge of murder.

seal: The wax marking on a contract to express serious consent. A contract under seal needs no special consideration.

sealed and delivered: A contract term indicating that the one who conveys has received consideration by delivery. Sealed gives added strength to the conveyance in terms of reinforced intent to convey.

search warrant: A court order giving a person the right to enter a specified building to search for specific objects.

searches: An examination of records before purchasing land to ensure that there are no incumbrances (*e.g.*, liens or easements).

S

secondary evidence: Not the best or most direct evidence. A witness who testifies as to the content of a written document gives secondary evidence. The document itself, if available, would be primary evidence.

section of land: A parcel of land of one square mile.

secured creditor: A creditor who has a special security for a debt (*e.g.*, a mortgage) which can be claimed in advance of the claims of general creditors.

security: A right to property or a fund to be used for satisfaction of a debt in the event that the debtor does not pay.

security for costs: A security to be given to the defendant during an action by the plaintiff to cover the defendant's costs.

sedition: The offense of publishing words or documents or making speeches to cause contempt of, or to undermine, the government. See **treason**.

seduction: The act of seducing. An action for damages in tort may be brought when a parent or master loses the services of a child or servant due to a debauching of their person.

seise, seize: To be put in possession of; to be aware or informed of something.

seisin: Formal legal ownership of land; taking possession of land.

S

self-defence: If a person uses reasonable force, under the circumstances, to defend himself and unintentionally kills another in so doing, the killing is excusable as an unintentional act.

selling price clause: A clause in an insurance contract to indicate loss settlement is based on an article's selling price rather than an insured's actual cost.

semble: It seems. Law which is not definite. Used in a law report to indicate an opinion of the court on a point not directly at issue.

sentence: The judgment of a court.

separation deed: A deed made between the separated husband and wife containing provisions for the dependent spouse and child.

separation order: An order given to a deserted spouse or one who has been assaulted.

sequester: To isolate or set apart (*e.g.*, as with a jury); setting apart a person's property for the benefit of creditors.

seriatum: Used in pleadings to deny specific allegations of the plaintiff, one by one, individually. See **counts.**

service: Bringing the contents or effect of a document to the notice of those involved; to serve with a writ of summons.

servient tenement: Land over which an easement runs in favour of the dominant tenement; land which is subject to the right of another. See **dominant tenement**.

S

servitium: Services.

servitude: An easement on land.

set back: An area a specified distance from an established line or curb on which buildings cannot be erected.

set-off: A cross-claim for money by a defendant in an action.

settle: To draft a contract and decide its terms; to make a settlement.

settled land: Land which is limited by way of succession to one person other than the person entitled to the land for the time being.

settlement: A deed settling property, as in a marriage settlement; the conclusion of a dispute between parties to an action; money exchanged between the parties to discharge liability.

settlement option: In insurance, there are often two or more ways of settling a claim. In life insurance a claim may be settled by a lump sum or by periodic payments of money over a certain length of time.

several: Separate.

severalty: To hold real property by one person alone with no other person having an interest. Compare with joint tenancy or tenancy in common.

severance: Division in a claim where parts can be acted upon separately; in real property, a process to sever a joint tenancy by partition.

S

share: A specific portion of the capital of a corporation. The holder is entitled to proportionate profits of the company.

share certificate: An instrument which states that the person owns a certain number of shares of a corporation.

sheriff: An officer of the court, usually a superior court, with varied duties such as execution of writs and, in some jurisdictions, having police powers.

shew cause, show cause: A rule of the court that a thing applied for be granted unless another party is able to show why it should not be granted.

shire: A county.

shire-reeve, shire clerk: A sheriff.

short date rates: If an insured requests cancellation of an insurance policy, the policy is cancelled short date; in excess of a *pro rata* proportion of the premium in order to cover additional costs of administration.

short title: A subsection of a statute setting out a simple abbreviated title for an act.

side track agreement: The owner of a factory holds a railway free of all liability for accidents on the portion of track the railway puts on the factory's premises. In insurance, coverage of this risk is quite common.

sign judgment: To enter formally the judgment of a court into the court record.

S

signature: A person's mark or name on a document signifying acceptance of the contents.

silent partner: See **dormant partner**.

simple contract: A contract, either express or implied, verbal or written, but not under seal.

sine die: Without date or without a day. An adjournment *sine die* is an adjournment of a hearing without signifying a day for resumption.

sine prole: Without issue.

single interest policy: An insurance policy where there is only one insured interest (*e.g.*, a nuclear insurance policy).

sittings in camera: Court hearings not in open court; in private.

skilled witness: An expert witness who gives evidence on a matter of which he has particular knowledge (*e.g.*, a handwriting expert).

slander: Defamation through words. See **defamation; libel**.

small claims courts: Courts hearing claims not exceeding a nominal sum set by statute. This affords inexpensive quick settlement and relieves higher courts of small claims.

smoke damage: For purposes of fire insurance, damage caused by smoke and not by the fire itself. It is covered by the fire insurance policy.

sodomy: Carnal knowledge *per* anus by a man upon the person of another man or woman. Can be used as grounds for divorce.

S

sole: Alone; single not married.

sole corporation: A corporation which is one person only, such as a queen or bishop. Such a corporation must sue or be sued in its corporate name.

solemn form probate: Solemn form probate is irrevocable by parties to it and is made in open court before all interested parties. Should a will post-dating the one proved be submitted later, the solemn form may be questioned and revoked on sufficient evidence of the validity of the new will.

solicitor: A lawyer. A person entitled to give legal advice or begin proceedings in court. See **attorney; barrister; counsel; lawyer**.

Solicitor-General: The Solicitor-General of Canada has authority to deal with federal legal matters, in particular, prisons, penitentiaries, parole, remissions, and the Royal Canadian Mounted Police. In the U.S.A., an officer of the department of justice, principal assistant to the Attorney General. See **Attorney-General**.

sound in damages, to: A phrase used in an action where damages are the relief sought.

speaker: The person who presides over a legislature and maintains order.

special administration: In estate matters, the administration of specific effects of the deceased.

special agent: One who acts for a principal for a particular purpose only and not in general.

S

special damage: Damages which must be expressly pleaded and proved to the court to gain compensation.

special examiner: One appointed by the court to examine and hear evidence for a special purpose to aid the court.

special hazards: In insurance, hazards which are not considered common and usual to a risk. Reference is generally to unusual or highly hazardous elements of the risk (*e.g.*, wood working plants possess special hazards in terms of potential combustion).

special property: A limited right to property; a person renting an automobile has a right to use it for a specific time for consideration.

specialty: A contract signed and under seal as distinct from a simple contract which is signed but not sealed.

specie: Payment in coin as distinct from payment in paper money; a payment in kind.

specific devise: A devise of specific real property.

specific performance: A remedy of a court sitting in equity to compel a defendant to perform the agreements in a contract. It is used where common law damages are not adequate for justice to be done the plaintiff.

spouse: A husband or wife.

stare decisis: To abide by precedents or decided cases that stand until changed in the legal process.

S

statement of adjustments: A statement, made by the solicitor for a vendor in a sale of land, in balance sheet form, so that on the closing of the sale both vendor and purchaser have an accurate record of all financial terms and settlements in the matter.

statement of claim: A written statement by the plaintiff showing the facts of a claim against a defendant.

statement of defence: A pleading in a court, opposing a statement of claim, made and filed by the defendant.

State's evidence: In the U.S.A., wherein an accomplice gives evidence in a criminal matter hoping for a pardon or light sentence. See **King's evidence**.

status: The legal condition of a person; one's capacity to make a contract or to institute legal proceedings; one's position in reference to citizenship.

status quo: The current state of things.

statute: Law as set by an act of the government.

Statute of Frauds: A statute requiring that certain contracts must be in writing to be enforceable by the courts (*e.g.*, matters with regard to land).

statutes of limitation: Statutes setting out the maximum periods of time in which an action must be commenced in court; keeping alive the right of a plaintiff to refer his claim to a court.

statutory declaration: A written statement of facts signed by the declarant before a magisterial officer declaring that the facts set forth are true.

S

stay of execution: The suspension of the operation of a judgment of the court.

stay of proceedings: Suspension of proceedings in an action, temporarily or permanently, if one of the involved persons does not comply with orders.

steal: To commit a theft of property belonging to another.

stirpes, distribution per: The division of property among families on intestacy, considering representatives of deceased persons who, if they had survived, would have taken a share of the property. See **capita, distribution per**.

stocks and shares: Issued to the owners of a corporation who then become shareholders entitled to share in profits.

stoppage in transitu: The right of an unpaid vendor to reclaim goods sold on credit until payment is received, as long as the goods are still in transit.

stranded: In marine insurance, a ship is stranded when it is driven onto shore by weather or poor navigation.

street offence: An offence able to be committed in a street (*e.g.*, soliciting for purposes of prostitution).

strict liability: A person is responsible for accidental harm regardless of negligence or intention to harm another.

sub judice: In the course of the trial, an issue now before the courts.

sub modo: Under a restriction or a condition.

S

sub nom. (sub nomine): Under the name.

sub voce: Under the title.

subject to contract: An offer made so that there is no contract until the final contract is executed.

subornation of perjury: Persuading a person to commit perjury.

subpoena: A writ issued requiring a person to be present at a specified place and time for a specific purpose.

subrogation: Substituting one person or thing for another so that the duties of the first person become the duties of the substituted person; the rights of an insurer who has paid a claim to assume all rights of the insured against the one who caused the loss.

subrogation release: A release taken by an insurer after indemnifying the insured taking over rights of subrogation. See **subrogation**.

subscribe: To apply for shares; to sign.

subscribing witness: A person who signs a legal instrument as attesting witness to another's execution of the instrument.

subscription policy: In fire insurance, a contract where two or more insurers subscribe to one policy a set amount each shown on the policy.

substituted service: Where legal process is served on one other than the one who should be served due to impossibility of personal direct service (*e.g.*, on an agent rather than a principal).

S

succession: When property passes, on death, from one person to a successor.

sue: To bring a civil action against a person.

suffrage: An elective franchise; a right to vote.

sui juris: A person who has full legal capacity.

suicide: To kill oneself.

suit: Legal proceedings brought by one person against another.

summary conviction offence: A lesser criminal offence, usually before a magistrate without a jury. See **indictable offence; misdemeanor**.

summing up: The speech by a judge to a jury in which the important points of a case are reviewed and in which directions needed are given.

summons: A document issued by the court ordering the person to appear before the judge.

superintendent of insurance: In Canada, the principal officer of the insurance department of the government whose function is to regulate insurance. See **insurance commissioner**.

superior courts: Courts of wide jurisdiction generally unlimited by statute. See **inferior court**.

suppliant: The claimant in a petition of right to obtain restitution for real or personal property from the government.

S

support: The right of a person to have land physically supported by a neighbor's land. It refers to lateral support which, if removed, is actionable in tort.

supra: Above. Generally refers a reader to a previous section of a book.

Supreme Court: The court of last resort. This court has civil and criminal jurisdiction both direct and on appeal.

surcharge: A charge levied or imposed on an existing charge; in insurance, a surcharge, or extra premium, may be added due to an increase in risk.

surety: A person who agrees to satisfy an obligation of another person.

surety bond: An agreement whereby a person or insurer (the surety) guarantees performance of one party (the principal) to the obligee (a party for whom the principal undertakes to do something).

surplus: A corporation's financial position; the amount by which assets exceed liabilities.

surrender: The moving of a lesser estate into a greater; surrender in deed is to yield up a life estate to a remainderman or a person with a reversion; giving up oneself to the authorities while a fugitive.

surrogate: A person substituted or appointed in the stead of another, particularly, substitution of the deputy of a bishop to grant marriage licences.

S

surrogate court: A court whose function is to supervise, approve and direct matters testamentary.

survivorship: The right of survivorship, the main characteristic of joint tenancy; to survive to an estate in land excluding rights of all others in a deceased's estate.

suspension: The temporary cessation of a law by proper authority; the temporary cessation of a person's office or job.

T

tangible property: Property which may be touched as compared to intangible rights. Land is tangible, copyright is intangible.

tariff: In insurance, a rate set by a rating bureau and charged by its members.

taxation: Duties levied to raise revenue.

taxing costs: The process of the court assessing the costs involved between the solicitor and client for work done by the solicitor.

tenancy in common: Two or more persons holding real property each with an undivided possessory interest. It may be transferred by alienation or devised by will. There are no rights of survivorship.

tenant: A person who possesses land; one who rents land or buildings.

tenant at will: A person who possesses land or buildings by lease until the owner requires their return.

tenant for life: A person who holds and uses buildings or land until death with the remaider in fee simple to a named beneficiary.

tender: An offer of money to satisfy an obligation; an offer to supply certain commodities.

tenement: A house, especially one with several different apartments. Something that is subject to tenure.

T

tenure: A system of holding land in relation to some superior right; the manner whereby a tenant, in feudal ages, was holden to a lord.

term insurance: Life insurance that is taken for a specific number of years only.

term of years: An interest in land limited to a set number of years.

testament: A person's will indicating how property should be distributed.

testamentary causes: Matters that the court must rule on with respect to the validity and execution of a will.

testate: A person who dies leaving a will. See **testator**.

testator/testatrix: A male/female person who has made a will.

testes, proof of will (per testes): The witnesses' proof of a will, in solemn form, where validity is questioned. See **solemn form probate**.

testimonium: The end of a will which reads, "In witness, etc.".

testimony: Evidence, given in court, by a witness.

theft: The taking, without lawful authority, of property of another.

theft (spouse): During cohabitation a husband or wife cannot be charged with theft of the property of the other.

T

third party: A person who is not directly involved in a transaction; not a party to a proceeding.

third party insurance: Insurance which indemnifies the insured for loss he may suffer for his legal liability to others.

third party release: A release between an insured and a third party, which acknowledges no further claim will be made.

ticket of leave: In the U.K., the practice of releasing a prisoner before the sentence is over. See **parole**.

time of the essence: If a time for completion of a contractual agreement is specified and is of the essence, non-performance by one party in that time entitles the other to consider the contract broken.

title: Evidence that a person is owner of personalty or realty.

title deeds: Documents proving ownership of land.

title insurance: A contract of guarantee that a title to land is free of any defects or encumbrances.

to have and to hold: Words in a deed which give estate to the grantee; known as the *habendum*.

Torrens System: A system of land holding and recording indicating ownership, encumbrances and title without further search of public records. The appropriate government guaranteeing the title to be accurate.

tort: A civil action excluding an action in contract; a civil right of action as in a motor vehicle accident.

tort feasor: A person who commits a tort.

tortious: A wrongful action by one party causing damage to another.

totidem verbis: In so many words.

trade fixture: In the nature of a chattel, but fixed to the premises. When a tenant has carried on a business and the lease expires, trade fixtures may be removed providing the realty is restored to its former condition. The fixtures are not part of the realty.

trade mark: A mark or signature fixed to an article to show that it is manufactured by a certain firm or person.

trade union: An organization of people who are involved in the same trade, established to facilitate negotiation of rights for the members.

transcript: A written or recorded copy of proceedings (*e.g.*, evidence).

transfer: Passing a right from one person to another.

traumatic injury: Physical injury rather than disease including psychological or emotional shock.

traverse: A denial of another person's claim of fact.

treason: An attempt to overthrow the government in power by transmitting information of military or scientific matters to another state. See **sedition**.

T

treasure trove: Money, gold, silver, etc., found hidden, the owner being unknown. In such case it belongs to the government or state. See **bona vacantia.**

treaty reinsurance: All insurance companies have a limit as to how much insurance they can provide for any risk. Over that amount reinsurance by treaty is needed. Under the amount, risks written by the prime company are automatically accepted, subject to agreed guidelines. Both share premiums and losses. See **facultative reinsurance**.

trespass: To enter without permission upon the land of another; to trespass the person (*e.g.*, assault, false imprison, etc.).

trespasser: A person who goes on another's land without permission.

trial: The examination and decision of a legal action before the court.

trial de nova: A new trial.

true bill: When a grand jury finds a charge against an accused to be valid a true bill is issued against the accused.

trust: Transfer of property to a person or corporation known as the trustee who holds the property for a person known as the beneficiary. See **cestui que trust**.

trustee: A person to whom an estate is conveyed in trust for another.

trustee in bankruptcy: The person who holds in trust the property of a bankrupt. The trustee's duty is to discover and distribute the property among creditors.

U

uberrima fides: Of the utmost good faith. Contracts are *uberrima fides* when the promisee must disclose every fact to the promisor; contracts in insurance are *uberrima fides*.

ubi jus, ibi remedium: Where there is a right, there is a remedy.

ultra vires: Beyond the power. An act which exceeds the law's power and is invalid. A province or state cannot legislate matters exclusive to the federal government or the matter will be *ultra vires*. See **intra vires**.

umpire: A third person appointed to make a decision in arbitration.

uncertainty: A deed or will may be void if it is drawn in an unclear manner and the court cannot interpret it.

unconscionable contract: One which is slanted so greatly to one side that a presumption of fraud or undue influence may arise.

undertaking: A promise which is enforceable in the same manner as an injunction.

undertaking to appear: A lawyer's promise to enter an appearance in court for a client.

underwriter: A person who enters with others into an insurance policy as insurer.

undivided share: Land which belongs to its owners jointly.

undue influence: Improper, unlawful pressure put on a person to benefit the one who pressures (*e.g.*, a will or contract in which undue influence is proved may be set aside).

U

unearned premium: Should an insurance policy be cancelled by an insurer before full term, that part of the premium not used or earned is returned to the insured.

unemployment insurance: A federal insurance scheme to make weekly payments to unemployed persons until new employment is obtained, or until the term of benefits lapses.

unenforceable: Something that cannot be sued on in the courts; a contract in an improper form, or containing an illegal object.

unilateral: One-sided, especially in contract law where only one party is bound.

union: A group of persons who join together for their common good, usually workers as opposed to employers.

uninsured motorist cover: If an insured plaintiff suffers automobile damage by an uninsured third party and the court gives judgment for the plaintiff, the plaintiff's insurer will make the payment of the judgment.

unity of possession: In order to create a joint tenancy in land there must be four unities of possession by the joint tenants: (1) all must take title at the same time; (2) all must have simultaneous possession; (3) all must have the same quantity of interest; (4) all must take title from the same person or persons. See **joint tenancy**.

unlawful assembly: A meeting of three or more people who are planning to commit a crime or breach of peace.

unliquidated: Not ascertained in amount; undetermined. Unliquidated damages must be determined by a jury.

U

unnamed insured: An insurance policy which covers not only the named insured but also others (*e.g.*, an automobile policy to cover anyone driving with the registered owner's permission).

unsatisfied judgment fund: A fund to pay for uninsured accidents, the money coming from uninsured motorists who pay a surcharge on vehicle registration, plus money from the provincial or state governments.

unsound mind: A person of unsound mind is mentally incompetent.

usage: Uniform conduct of people in one matter.

user: The enjoyment of property.

uses, deed to: A form of land conveyance to a man to prevent a wife's right to dower.

usufruct: A right to enjoy the use of another's property, but having no right to destroy or lay it waste.

usury: Excessive and illegal interest rates.

uterine: Born of the same mother, but having different fathers.

uttering: Using a forged document knowing it is false. See **forgery**.

uxor: Wife; abbreviated to "ux." in a common expression "John Doe et ux.".

uxoricide: The killing of a wife by her husband.

V

v. or vs.: Versus. Used in citations of legal actions (*e.g.*, *Smith v. Jones*).

vacant possession: Premises sold not subject to leases and thus vacant for the possession and use by the purchaser.

vagabond or vagrant: A wanderer, or idle person. Persons without visible means of support.

valid: That which has binding force recognized by law.

valuable consideration: The passing of something of value between parties to a contract for performance of the contract. It may be a right, forebearance, interest, or profit.

value: The cost of replacing an article lost or destroyed. In insurance, it is determined after allowing for depreciation, wear, tear, etc.

valued insurance policy: One in which the parties agree at the time of issuing the policy as to the value of the insured property.

vandalism: Intended damage to property.

variance: A discrepancy between a material statement in a pleading and the evidence, or between a writ and a pleading.

vendor: A seller, usually of land. In the sale of goods this person is actually called the seller.

vendor's lien: A claim a vendor has on title until all money still owing is received. Often called a mortgage back.

venereal disease: Social diseases such as syphilis, gonorrhea, or soft chancre.

V

venue: The place of a trial. In a criminal case venue may be changed to avoid local prejudice in jurors. See **removal of action**.

verdict: The decision of a jury in a proceeding.

versus: Against. In the title of a case before the court it indicates the plaintiff against the defendant. See **v. or vs**.

vest: To deliver, or convey, full possession of land or rights to another; to clothe with legal rights.

vested in interest: An estate is vested in interest when possession of property will be in the future; a reversion of the property.

vested in possession: An estate is vested in possession when immediate possession of property is given.

vesting instrument: A vesting deed, or order.

vesting order: An order of the court where property is passed to another, usually in matters of land.

vexatious actions: A proceeding in which the party who is bringing the action is doing it only to bother and annoy the opponent.

vi et armis: With force and arms.

vicarious liability: Liability imposed, by law, on a person though he is not involved in an occurence; an automobile owner is liable vicariously for injury caused by a person driving his auto with his permission.

vinculo matrimonii: From the bond of marriage.

V

vis major: Uncontrolled force; during hostilities with an enemy force, one may be relieved from a contract. See **act of God**.

viva voce: By word of mouth. Oral evidence given in court.

void: Having no force or effect; a nullity in law.

voidable: A transaction capable of being avoided or confirmed as compared to void.

voire dire: To speak the truth. A preliminary examination to determine the competency of a witness to give evidence.

volenti non fit injuria: Assumption of risk. An act is not actionable if the person assented to the act.

voluntary: Without valuable consideration.

voluntary confession: A confession made by the accused without threat or promise to the accused by a person in authority. Such a confession is admissible evidence.

voucher: A receipt which discharges the obligations of a debtor and which is evidence of payment.

W

wage: A salary; to give a security for the performance of something.

wager: A promise to give money or something of value when the result of an uncertain act is determined. A bet.

wages: Money paid by a master to servants for services rendered.

waiver: Forsaking a right or interest; to renounce or abandon a claim which may be expressed or implied.

war clause: Clauses in insurance contracts purporting to relieve an insurance company of liability should loss occur because of war.

ward: An infant who is under the care of a guardian.

warden: A guardian, or person, who has custody of another (*e.g.*, a prison warden).

warehouse receipt: A document of title to goods in a warehouse.

warrant: An authority under seal used in civil and criminal cases to execute process, to produce evidence or arrest a person.

warranty: An assurance, or guarantee. In the sale of goods, a promise that that which is sold belongs to the vendor and is suitable for the purpose for which the purchaser intends to use it. It is essentially a guarantee.

wasting assets: Property with a limited existence; a lease on property.

W

water course: The right of a person to the benefit of an unrestricted flow of a stream or river.

way, right of way: The right to pass over another person's land.

way-bill: A document listing persons or property in charge of a public carrier.

wear and tear: Deterioration arising from ordinary, reasonable use of a thing; the waste and damage normally found in using such a thing. Often in leases, ordinary wear and tear is allowed of a tenant.

weight of evidence: When the evidence at a hearing leans to one party and the jury finds in favour of the other party, the verdict has gone against the weight of evidence.

whole blood: The relationship between two persons descended from two common ancestors (same mother and father) as opposed to half blood (same mother or father, but not both).

will: The disposition or declaration of a person providing for the distribution of property after death. It is revocable anytime prior to death.

winding-up: The ending or stopping of a company, or partnership, and settling of all accounts.

withdrawal: The withdrawal or discontinuance of the plaintiff's claim in an action.

without prejudice: A statement given without prejudice cannot be construed as admission of liability or admitted in evidence. It is used in pre-trial negotiations between counsels when attempting to settle a dispute out of court.

W

witness: A person who, under oath, gives evidence in a matter; a person who subscribes his name to a document to attest to its validity and execution.

workman's compensation: A law whereby an employee injured in the course of employment receives compensation whether the employer is liable or not. Generally the worker receives medical payments and a proportion of wages based on disability. This replaces one's common law right to sue an employer for damages.

writ: A written instrument requiring the person named to comply with its provisions.

writ of assistance: A specific writ to a law officer to do a particular thing; *e.g.*, in some jurisdictions used with respect to narcotic violations; in others re: illegal land possession.

writ of summons: Issued by the court to give a defendant notice of a claim against him.

write: In insurance, the underwriting or acceptance of a risk by an insurer.

Y

year to year: Used in reference to an annual leasehold interest in land.

yellow dog contract: A contract in labor law in which the employee agrees not to join a labor union.

yield: Monetary returns from an investment; surrendering possession of an estate.

young person: A person under eighteen years of age, having no legal capacity.

Z

zone: An area in municipal regulation set aside for certain purposes.

zoning laws: The by-laws or regulations of a municipality to control certain land areas for specific reasons.